Soul Searching

Get on Board for TRANSFORMATION

Using The TAPIN Method

by

Brenda Warren

Copyright (C) 2022 by Brenda Warren

Cover Design by: Valentina
TAPIN Illustration by: Alex Warren

Disclaimer
ALL RIGHTS RESERVED. This book contains material protected under International and Federal Copyright Laws and Treaties. Any Unauthorized reprint or use of this material is prohibited. No part of this book may be reproduced or transmitted in any form or by any means, electronic or mechanical, including photocopying, recording, or by any information storage and retrieval system, without express written permission from the author/publisher.

Notice of Liability
All the material contained in this book is provided for educational and informational purposes only. No responsibility can be taken for any results or outcomes resulting from the use of this material. While every attempt has been made to provide information that is both accurate and effective, the author does not assume any responsibility for the accuracy or use/misuse of this information.

Websites and Ideas
The Internet is a fluid changing medium and websites change all the time. All links are for information purposes only and are not warranted for content, accuracy or any other implied or explicit purpose.
The ideas expressed in this book are my own and there are no guarantees that you will have success with them. This book is intended to be informational and is my opinion only. Please consider leaving a review wherever you brought the book or telling your friends about it.

ISBN: 979-8-7853-500-45

Publisher: Talk To ME Publishing
www.brendathesoulutionist.com

Amazon Author Central Page
https://www.amazon.com/author/brendathesoulutionist

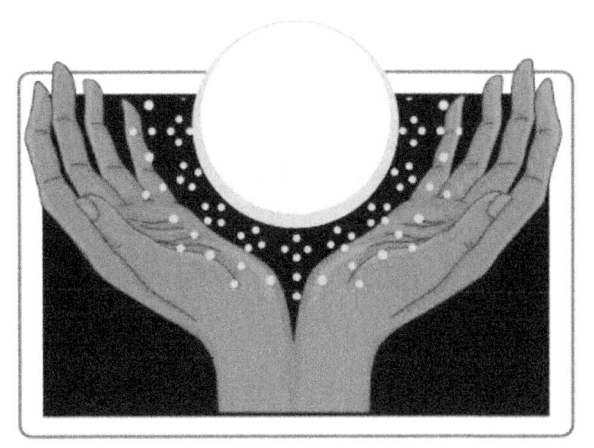

The Soulutionist
BRENDA WARREN

Dedication

This book is dedicated to my late mother, Minnie Lancaster, who believed I would make a difference in this world, and my nonbinary kiddo, Alex, who continues to redefine themself daily. I am so proud to be their mom.

To Magic for seeing me when I did not see myself. You fueled the stories that kept me sane when my world was falling apart. My love on paper that I will soon be sharing with the world. Your time is near.

To the Military men and women worldwide standing in the gap, I thank you. To my fellow Veterans, thank you for your service. To all the fallen heroes, past and present, you will never be forgotten. To the family members that have supported all of us, I am forever grateful for your sacrifice.

To all who can no longer lift their voice, I promise to continue working to prevent any more unnecessary silences.

Thank you to the men and women who read the first edition and asked questions while forming book clubs and reading groups in over seven different countries. This edition filled in the gaps and answered the questions you submitted.

To my now very close friend, fellow veteran, and accountability buddy Lisa Ducharme, I say thank you. Without her guidance, kicks in the butt, and constant, unwavering encouragement, this second edition would have never seen the light of day.

To all the people ready to **TAPIN** to *YOUR* best life ever while living their lives unapologetically unstoppable!

Acknowledgment

I would like to thank God for never giving up on me. Even when I was deep in my mess, he continued to send people to guide me into the light. I now understand that all the trials in my Life have prepared me for this moment in time. It takes a village! I thank those listed and unlisted for their support.

My family Aunt Elaine, Junie, and Bruce thank you for loving me.

Additionally, there are women that, without them, this book would have never even seen the light of day. Dee Hill and Bonita Jenkins, these women, bring great joy and richness to my Life. Their Godly counsel and friendship over the years have never failed. They have cried with and for me, prayed me through the most challenging times in my Life. Both have been sounding boards to me with open hearts without judgment. I will be forever grateful that God placed these mighty women of God in my Life.

From that day in the Service Center when you interviewed for a job, Julie Cusimano Wall, you changed my Life. You have been a friend, confidant, and editor when I could not even put a sentence together. How you view the world has made unique written and real-life journeys fun. Your belief in my ability to tell a story gave me the courage to pursue my writing passion. Here is the remix (smile).

Debbie Seagroves taught me about the box and to seek to understand before trying to be understood. Thank you for your willingness to stand in the gap, even when it was not easy even now.

Tonya Strickland-Utley, for all the pictures you made for me, including the inspiration for the original book's cover concept and your never-ending encouragement from the first time we met.

Lisa Ducharme and Marqueta Plum Jenkins, my power team, my personal Board of Directors, you have impacted my Life in ways that will not be erased. We have grown a lot since the first book.

Jen Gottlieb and Chris Winfield of Super Connector Media created an environment that allowed me to BE SEEN!!!!!! Chris and Jen, you indeed are my unfair advantage! I will be forever grateful for your continued support of all the Alumni of the Be On TV Challenge, the Been Seen Accelerator 3.0, Unfair Advantage Live and Super Connector Mastermind.

Liz Clarke of Tonya Bardo Boutique, you gave me wings, and now I am flying. Dawn and Freddy S. at the Brooklyn Café TV Show, thank you for believing in me and seeing something I did not see in myself. I will always be grateful for your generosity. Allowing me to sit at The Editor's Desk is an unbelievable dream come true.

Pete M. Lucas of Balancingbeems.com for his message of inner peace. For introducing me to the "M" word. For being my lyrical match. Thank you for teaching me more about journaling while sharing your outline as a framework in this book and being a true friend. Now with the beautiful soul of Lina by your side, you are truly unstoppable!

Michael Harper of Harper's Sports Performance, my trainer. Thank you for your continued encouragement and for not giving up on me when others would not even try despite my physical limitations.

Nicholas Anderson is a sounding board and always provides a word from God right when needed. Thank you, my friend. Your Next!

Mother Frankie Mae Bride, for all your words of wisdom, you believed in me when I did not believe in myself. The entire Williams Family for loving me from Camp Pendleton to here.

Perry and Kathleen Jenkins for all the love they have shown my family. Thank you for your continued support during this update.

Pastor Mercy Myles-Jenkins for answering the voice of God for other women and me. May God bless you a thousandfold for ensuring our stories would be heard and not stay locked inside ourselves.

Success leaves clues! Thank you, Megan Bendtzen, Patrice Francois, Mandeep Kaur, Dr. Jennifer Price, and Dr. Denise Sincere, for your friendship, personal, and professional development support. You ladies have each demonstrated a level of excellence that makes me very proud to be a part of your circle.

Sandi Masori, your support of this second edition played a significant role in becoming a bestseller. Your kindness and support will never be forgotten.

Finally, The Gift Activator, Coach D-EMMANUEL, held my hand even when it was not easy. You believed this second edition would reach bestseller status on Amazon, and it did in five categories. You are a blessing.

THANK YOU

When I joined the United States Marine Corps on June 10, 1980, I had no way of knowing how that would forever change my life. I traveled worldwide, learned many valuable lessons, and found out I am much more robust than I ever dreamed possible. I formed many friendships that will last a lifetime.

Combat claimed many; some have made it to ripe old ages. Still, others fell victim to the unnecessary silence, currently claiming our Veterans to this day. I want to be a voice for the voiceless. I never want to fail to acknowledge the sacrifice of the men, women, and their families that serve in our Nation's Military.

To all my fellow Veterans, I say thank you. To the Men & Women serving, have served, those who gave their lives that we all may be safe, and their families that have endured much while they protected us all, I say thank you. My family and I thank you all for your Service and continue to pray for your families.

I pray for God's blessing over our military and our Nation. Our Country will never forget the fallen as long as we celebrate their memory. The living still has time to thank our service members for the sacrifices they make daily. Wounded Warriors (seen & unseen), your cries are heard. Today and every day, my family and I honor you all. May God give a special blessing to all that have served, and May God Bless America.

THANK YOU

TABLE OF CONTENTS

Thank You ix
Foreword by Dan Tricarico... xiii
Introduction xvii
SECTION ONE 21
    Chapter 1_What Is Soul Searching?....................................... 23
    Chapter 2_The Soul Search 35
    Chapter 3 The Seven Why's... 41
    Chapter 4_Travelers' Core Beliefs... 45
    Chapter 5 Soul Searching Exercise 53
SECTION TWO 69
    Chapter 6 What is TAPIN?... 71
    Chapter 7 TRANSFORMATION - Tell Yourself Something Good to Transform Your Mind 78
    Chapter 8__Announcement and Accountability – Announce YOUR Intentions and Be Accountable 86
    Chapter 9 Preparation - Prepare For Your Desired Outcome 90
    Chapter 10 Imagination - Visualize You Are Already in Possession of Your Change 96
    Chapter 11 Nurture – Cultivate Your Dream........................ 100
    Chapter 12 How to Apply TAPIN to your Life 104
    Chapter 13 Sample TAPIN's 108
    Chapter 14 Well-Balanced Unapologetically Unstoppable Life.... 138
    Chapter 15 Finding Your Voice.. 142
    Chapter 16 My Fellow Veterans 148
About the Author 161
BONUS 162
ADDITIONAL RESOURCES 164

Foreword by
DAN TRICARICO

Once upon a time I wanted a guitar. I had learned how to play a bit when I was in high school and I wanted to try again. And even though I couldn't afford a guitar at the time, I kept imagining myself strumming the strings late at night in my room and playing my favorite songs from my childhood and teen years. For a long time, the fantasies of playing and singing distracted me from the bumps and challenges of my life. As a result, I often found myself thinking, "If I only had a guitar, THEN I would be happy."

So I saved and I saved. I secreted away birthday money, sold stuff, turned in aluminum cans for change, and did anything I could to slip some cash into the envelope in the cupboard marked "GUITAR." And one day, after I counted up a whopping $100, I went into a local pawnshop one day after work and I bought a guitar for $80.

It was beautiful.

It had a long, lean neck, a beautiful body, and a deep, resonant sound.

I finally had my guitar. And I loved it.

At this point, you might think this is a story about how I believed in myself, took decisive action, and manifested something that I wanted.

Not exactly.

The thing is: I bought the guitar, brought it home, and everything was. .

Exactly the same.

I still had the same challenges. The same frustrations. And all those danged bumps were still in EXACTLY the same places.

Not only had nothing changed, but I really wasn't any happier than I was before I entered the pawn shop.

Buying that guitar taught me a very important lesson, though...

Stuff doesn't make us happy.

I was a grown adult, and mostly mature in every sense of the word. And yet I didn't realize that simply owning a guitar would never make me happy. That experience taught me that happiness comes from inside. I learned that true joy is a function of simplicity, peace, and aligning your life choices with your value and belief systems.

It's also about having a purpose.

And that's where Brenda Warren comes in.

Brenda will be the first to tell you she has had some challenges in her life and that happiness has sometimes been elusive. She may have been down, but she's never been out. Over time, she has overcome those obstacles, stepped into her power and greatness, and now she is shining her light brightly over all of us. Overcoming her obstacles was a win for Brenda, but it was also a win for us because now all of us can benefit from her wisdom.

In short, she has found her reason for being on this earth.

She has found her purpose.

And now, in the pages of this book, she's going to share how to do that for yourself.

Soul Searching: Get on Board for Transformation Using the TAPIN Method is a powerful book that outlines Brenda's signature process for meeting your needs, reaching your goals, and finding your purpose.

Do you want to know why you were put on this earth?

Do you want to reach goals you never thought possible?

Do you want to discover reserves of strength, hope, and imagination you never knew you possessed?

Then keep reading.

Brenda Warren's signature TAPIN Method is a great process for discovering why you're here and for living for (and in) a greater purpose than for the status quo, Merry-Go-Round, hamster wheel existence most of us find ourselves in. It will show you how to invest in something greater than yourself. Warren's process helps us figure out what's important to us, what drives us, and what we are meant to do while we're here on this earth.

Your purpose, for example, just might be playing guitar.

Or it might not.

To find out, you'll need to TAPIN.

The TAPIN can take you from where you are to where you want to go.

And one more thing:

Always remember that Happiness is an inside job.

Dan Tricarico

Author**, *The ZEN Teacher***: *Creating Focus, Simplicity, and Tranquility in the Classroom, and* **Sanctuaries***: SELF-CARE SECRETS FOR STRESSED-OUT TEACHERS*

Dan helps teachers and businesspeople reduce their stress, improve their self-care, and avoid burnout so they can thrive in the classroom, in the office, and in life. Connect with Dan at:

https://www.thezenteacher.com

INTRODUCTION

Welcome Traveler! Yes, that is you. Throughout Soul Searching, I will be referring to readers and clients that have already taken this trip as a Traveler. I am using the term Traveler to account for those who have already taken this adventure. Also, this term is used in anticipation of those willing to take this journey with me to find their voice while seeking to live an unapologetically unstoppable well-balanced life. The journey to self-discovery can take many paths. Our souls long to find our purpose; finding mine was an adventure filled with many detours. I have discovered there are many ways one may choose to reach their desired destination. It can be incredibly challenging when you are unsure how to get there.

This book is a two-part guide. Section One; Soul Searching, and Section Two is the step-by-step TAPIN Method. Each unit stands separately or as a combined tool. In the TAPIN Chapters, some information has been repeated, making them self-contained teaching modules for ease of use. Affirmations to strengthen your midset shift have been added to this edition for additional support.

I believe determining where you want to go is the key to reaching your intended location. The gap between your starting point and desired ending destination can be the scariest part of your journey. Once you decide to make the trip, how do you get there? The decision to travel made, you must now get clear on your vehicle of choice.

Planning a soul searching trip can be easily derailed if not adequately thought through. Personal limitations combined with an improper transportation choice is a recipe for disaster. In this book/journal, you will be Soul Searching while using the TAPIN Method. The TAPIN Method is a five-step strategic process designed to help you get clear on what you want: Transform, Announce/Accountability, Prepare, Imagine and Nurture. Together we will be taking an imaginary trip to Grandma's house.

There was no better place to soul search when I was a child than while sitting on Nana's Lap. She was full of Godly wisdom. She always had a way of making things clear. The colorful stories she wove made my imagination soar. The flawed characters in her life lessons always seem to triumph in the end. The love and guidance she provided would make a lasting impression. Her tales would cement a strong foundation for a life destined to encounter many twists, turns, and detours.

If you are ready, I ask you to join me as we travel on an adventure. Our trip will make a few stops; take you along for some of the actual detours of my Life. I will always direct you back on track helping you find your ticket to live an unapologetically unstoppable, well-balanced life. Initially, I will be your guide on this trip; sometimes, it helps to have a road map. However, I must warn you that you may not complete this trip even with my life as a guide. Soul Searching is not for the faint-hearted. It takes time, patience, and the ability to unpack luggage you may not even have known you had acquired. Be assured that if you stay the course, you will be able to soul search with confidence with practice.

By the end of this adventure, you will be able to take this trip repeatedly as needed. It is a trip that will allow you to see things differently each time you take it—never losing sight of your desire to maintain balance. We are not looking for perfection. We are looking to take an honest trip allowing you to see all the possibilities unfold before your eyes as you soul search. I hope you will even invite someone else to take the journey with you on occasion. The best part of any journey is the discovery. However, how you get there can often make or break your trip.

As an example, I live in beautiful Goldsboro, North Carolina. Travelers brave enough to get in an actual vehicle I am driving have considered me a distracted driver. Not safe for me or others on the road. We are about to take our trip to visit my Grandma in Wilmington, Delaware. We have the option to travel by boat, airplane, automobile, or train. All are excellent sources of transportation. The question is which one is the right choice for our trip. I have decided we will take the Train.

With its many cars, a train glides its way down a predetermined set of tracks designed to guide us to our correct destination every time without fail. Sometimes, there can be stops along the way. Multiple strategically placed platforms exist along the route of the track. Each one will allow Travelers to take a break, sight-see, and even end their trip if warranted. These stopping points ensure we can get right back on track and continue to our intended destination as we choose.

Over the years, Soul Searching using the TAPIN Method has facilitated previous Travelers with uncovering their ultimate "why." Many Travelers became clear regarding their core values and set solid spiritual practices. Others increased happiness, improved relationships, and fitness levels while they developed better eating habits.

Travelers have reported financial enhancements, professional development increases that had eluded them in the past. A few select Travelers pursued their entrepreneurial dreams after Soul Searching using the TAPIN Method.

Additionally, many Veterans have been able to apply the practices outlined among these pages to help them manage stress and utilize their military skill set to excel in the civilian sector.

Accomplishing some or all the above is possible if you choose to take the journey with an open heart. After completing Soul Searching, Some Travelers may only need to land on one or two platforms to complete their journey. The Soul Searching section alone may be enough to get them on track.

Other Travelers will not finish the soul search, finding it too difficult to continue the trip at this time. Fortunately, this is a self-paced trip. Travelers may continue their journey whenever time and temperament permits.

Remaining Travelers will decide to continue with the complete trip. Each Traveler gets to choose how much of the journey they take and in which order. I always tell Travelers, "Life is choice-driven; the choices you make today will be the reality you live tomorrow. Choose wisely."

Think of this book/journal as a roadmap to getting you where you want to go with the flexibility to take a break if needed. Let me help you design a lifetime trip that will transform how you travel through life. Are you prepared to take the journey?

I would like to be your Conductor, a friendly guide of sorts as you begin Soul Searching and Get on Board for TRANSFORMATION using the TAPIN Method. I promise it is a trip worth taking and one that you will never forget.

There is a quote by PLATO. "The life which is unexamined is not worth living." Soul Searching will allow you to examine your life and determine what you *really want* if you are willing to take the trip. Your adventure starts as soon as you turn the page.

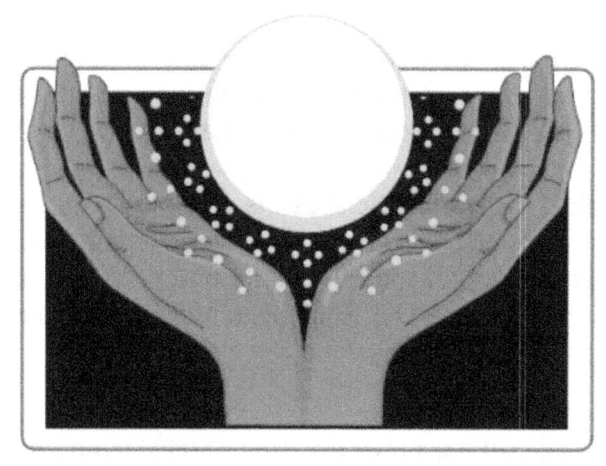

The Soulutionist
BRENDA WARREN

Let's Jump the Track to your Transformation

SECTION ONE

Soul Searching

"Soul Searching is a lifelong practice that I repeat regularly. It allows me to stay grounded. It helps me TAPIN, keeping me clear on my intentions and purpose."

-Brenda Warren

Chapter 1

What Is Soul Searching?

> *"A Soul unleashed is a force to be reckoned with."*
> *- Brenda Warren*

The Soul has been described as a driver in the body. Many religions support the belief that the Soul and spirit are one. They contend the Soul is the spark that gives us life. I started using the term "Soulutionist" as a way to describe what I did when I worked with individuals. I was helping people create new patterns for living, incorporating a mind, body, and soul approach unique to their personal needs. With everything within me I wanted myself and others to live fully fulfilled, fully expressed unapologetically unstoppable lives! I desired that people stop apologizing for living their best life.

The process begins by requesting each Traveler to share what they want to get out of the sessions and why they want it. Asking these questions laid a foundation for us to build goals to accomplish their most pressing issue. Some Travelers informed me it was the first time they had ever been asked, "What do you want." Additionally, most had never been asked, "why?"

They were learning to find and use their authentic voices. I discovered the spiritual base (or lack thereof) central to their success with each encounter. It was clear to me that no matter what a person's religious beliefs, we all need to soul search at some point in life. Soul Searching is looking for that deeper meaning inside oneself. It is how we each establish or clarify our core beliefs. It is an opportunity to discover what really matters to us, above all else.

During a soul search, Travelers are encouraged to consider:

- Spiritual foundations
- Mental health and their current belief system
- Their physical fitness, health, and wellness needs
- Financial freedom possibilities
- Professional development opportunities, to include entrepreneurship, if desired
- Veterans are asked to review their military experiences
- Their ability to speak authentically

Your pattern for living develops using these evaluations. My approach to helping Travelers craft a well-balanced, unapologetically unstoppable life and design patterns for living using a mind-body-soul method in its entirety.

Voiceless Travelers with voices stolen from them due to abuse in adulthood or being forced to remain silent as a child will find this exercise brings freedom. No matter what the soul search uncovers, the trip you are about to take will help you get on track.

Travelers are often confused and tired by the time I need to punch their tickets. Some have even arrived and gotten comfortable in their seat only to realize they do not even have their passports. However, once onboard this Train, my job is to ensure they can safely arrive at the desired destination.

When working with a new Traveler, to make a change in any area, it was essential to allow them the freedom to plan a unique itinerary. Designing a custom route would be the key to producing the change we expected. Once I started to deal with the heart and soul of the matter, everything changed. In my business, I get to meet many different types of travelers. A Traveler unsure why they were taking a trip could find themselves taking it repeatedly due to lack of direction.

The *Seven Steps to Why* will be our starting point of this journey.

The Seven Steps to Why is a critical process for your soul search. You will do this exercise in Chapter 3. It will bring focus and begin the getting real with yourself portion of your journey. It is paramount each Traveler is committed to the journey, not just interested. Let's take a look at a few types of travelers:

Interested Travelers would often board the Train. They would occasionally purchase first-class seating. They would announce boldly to the world they were taking the trip. Interested Travelers have been known to buy a new wardrobe to maximize their styling and profiling during the journey. Once the trip has started, they will get on and off the Train, making excuses or complaining about how long the journey was taking. Interested travelers rarely finish the trip, blaming everyone but themselves for ending their journey.

Frequent Travelers travel non-stop. They will take trips at the drop of a hat, without concern for the destination. Frequent Travelers will always sit in the front seat and take in all the sights. They brag to all their friends about all the trips they have taken. Once the trip is over, they have nothing to show for their perpetual journeys but stress and bills. Worst of all, they cannot even remember what the trip was about or where they went.

Committed Travelers are my favorite passengers. These are the ones that do not care where they sit. They are simply happy to be on the Train. They have not necessarily planned for the trip yet are looking forward to it. A committed traveler will exit the Train occasionally go sightseeing. The difference is this Traveler will ALWAYS return and continue the journey because they understand it takes time to get where they are going. If you are reading this, I will venture to say you are a committed traveler.

Traveling Style:

What type of Traveler are you at this moment; interested, frequent, committed, or none of the above?

_____

_____

What type of Traveler would you like to be?

_____

_____

Document Your Travels with Journaling!

Journaling compels you to think about and process your Soul Search. When you write about an experience or desire, you automatically process your dreams through words and description. Recording your thoughts in writing can lead you to notice details you hadn't seen. While journaling, put aside other ideas and focus on the soul search. It is a time to let your imagination soar. Imagine the life you want to live unapologetically unstoppable.

I recommend you have notepaper, pad, or separate journal to make additional notes. Journaling is an integral part of soul searching and the TAPIN Method. Writing out your thoughts and feelings will aid you in problem-solving. It will help you bring clarity to your desires. Additionally, it is a great way to track your progress and growth. There is no right or wrong approach to journaling. It is all up to you how you decide to capture your thoughts. Some Travelers will write longhand; others use a digital method, voice or written. If you do not currently journal, please consider making it a practice. I hope you will continue journaling after you have completed this book. It has been a lifelong adventure for me that helps reduce stress.

Some typical Journal types include:

- **Spiritual Journal:** Take note of your spiritual experiences

- **Fitness Journal**: Notate exercise so you can stay committed to a healthy, active lifestyle

- **Food Journal:** Track your eating to lose weight, gain muscle or maintain healthy eating habits

- **Gratitude Journal:** Express your feelings of thankfulness

- **Dream Journals:** Write out your dreams each morning as a way of getting in touch with your subconscious, or if you awaken immediately after your dream, you can keep a notebook by the bed and jot down your dream before rolling over and going back to sleep
- **Stream of consciousness:** Write down your thoughts as they happen. The words and ideas do not have to make sense; you are only writing out your thoughts and actions

The list above is not all-inclusive. It is a sample of the many ways journaling can be applied as a daily practice if you choose to do so. I use a combination of all of these journaling practices in my everyday life. I have been journaling since I was a child. Writing in my journal is like talking to a friend. It is a safe place to record my deepest darkest secrets and my ultimate dreams. You will have the opportunity to use some of the above styles throughout this book. If you are new to journaling, this sample outline and entry may help you with developing your own unique practice:

Sample Journal Outline:

Date: MM/DD/YYYY

Gratitude:

What are you grateful for? Start with the names of people and use family, friends, groups, spirituality, professions; be specific.

Take it to the next level by writing something in gratitude for someone you have negative feelings toward. Writing it out is a great way to work toward forgiveness.

Power Statement:

Write statements that make you feel empowered.

Affirmations:

Write positive statements or mantras in their completed states.

Reflections:

Why did I get so worked up about this today?

Why do I care about what others think?

How did today's problems reveal my character?

Sample Journal Entries:

Date: 00/00/0000

Gratitude:

I am grateful for loving family and friends.

I am thrilled to walk in forgiveness toward those that hurt me.

Power Statement:

All my desires are being fulfilled, and I retain the abundance to help others.

I am the manifestation of limitless potential.

Affirmations:

Each day I develop & enhance my *mental* capabilities with new learning.

My physical *body* reflects a lifestyle of conscious choices for health and wellbeing.

My *spiritual* connection is grounded in devotion, commitment, and practice.

Love is the conduit for manifesting limitless possibilities.

Reflections (End of the Day):

I am still working on understanding "hurt people, hurt people."

I am still working on not being a people pleaser.

I did not lash out when I was hurt.

Journaling inside and outside of this book will have a powerful impact on your life. Journaling is different for every person; your outcomes will vary. Your writing can provide positive feedback to help with decision-making during your soul search. As you work through each journaling prompt area, remember there is no right or wrong answer. Keep a journal if you are truly serious about soul searching and using the TAPIN Method.

Use the following list to prepare for your journey:

- ✓ Keep an Open Mind. You may need to let go of some paradigms during this journey.
- ✓ Pen, Pencil or Electronic Capture Device
- ✓ Fresh unused Journal or notepad
- ✓ Comfortable seating
- ✓ A quiet place to prevent distractions
- ✓ Drink and snack of choice (it may take a while)
- ✓ You will need a minimum of thirty minutes per section to devote to the exercises ahead.
- ✓ Anything that will put you in the right frame of mind to do these exercises

Now that you have gathered all your tools and created a great environment. Keep them handy you will need them when you arrive in Chapter 5. It will be time to do a Soul Search. We are heading to our next stop. However, before we go, I have left space for you in different places to record your thoughts as you take this journey. Taking notes is a way to reinforce what you have learned. Take the time to ponder what you believe you will get from the soul searching exercise. Review your findings after you complete your soul search. Have you gained any new insights? Remember, there is no wrong answer.

"When I journal, I give myself permission to be free. The page holds no judgement. It allows me to place everything I feel unfiltered. Over the years, I have watched myself stumble, fall, and get back up without the disapproval or praise of the world. It has been life-changing." – *Brenda Warren*

Practice Journal Outline:

Date: _____

Gratitude: _____

_____

_____

Power Statement: _____

_____

_____

Affirmations: _____

_____

_____

Reflections (End of the Day): _____

_____

_____

NOTES:

"The Page Is A Blank Canvas I Don't Fear Filling, Because It Holds No Judgement."

-Brenda Warren

Chapter 2

The Soul Search

> *"A Soul is a divine gift. Nurturing your Soul is vital for your spiritual growth. Feed it as if your life depends on it."*
> *- Brenda Warren*

All aboard!!! Time to let it go. Unfortunately, this is where I may lose a few travelers. In my coaching practice, I started asking each brave Soul that wanted to travel with me to disconnect from social media as part of my Self-Care Saturday and Soul Searching Sunday routines. During this journey, I would like to request you do the same. Disconnecting from social media at least twice a week will allow you to clear your thoughts. I encourage each Traveler to obtain a separate journal for the soul-searching process. The pages in this book will not be enough to continue this practice. After the initial deep dive, the soul searching process should become a regular ritual. Each Traveler will determine the continuing frequency of daily/weekly/monthly. For maximum effect, soul searching should not be considered a one-time event. I conduct a personal soul search quarterly to ensure I remain on track. Soul searching is a lifelong practice that helps you maintain balance.

As your Conductor along this Journey, I will be here to assist you with all your travel needs. Firstly, visualize a passenger train; there is an engine, often many different types of cars, and perhaps even a caboose that makes the train complete. Platforms are the stops we make along the way. The train car and platforms comprise everything you need to eventually create a living pattern based on a mind, body, and soul approach. Travelers can decide which spiritual, mental, physical, financial, or professional areas need to be adjusted.

You may even want to explore becoming an entrepreneur. Additionally, if you are a Veteran dealing with the transition to civilian life, express those thoughts during your soul search.

As you conduct your soul search, imagine your life the way you want it to be. What is your relationship to what you believe is the higher power? What type of person do you want to be? What are your hopes and dreams? What would make you feel your life has a purpose? How do you want to show up in this world? Where do you want to live? What type of relationships do you want to have with associates, friends, family, partner, and your spouse? What kind of relationship do you want to have with your body? If you have an illness, chronic or otherwise, how can you deal with it? What is your relationship with money? What type of career do you want? Do you want to be an Entrepreneur? What self-care practices do you␣what to incorporate into your life? What can you celebrate in your life? How would you like your daily routine to look? During your soul search, meditate on these questions and any that you think are appropriate as you journal.

Be sure to seek professional help as needed. Some of the things you uncover may trigger emotions you may need resources to process. I want you to be safe. Pay attention to how your body, mind, and soul respond during this process. Soul searching, when done authentically, will challenge your belief systems and patterns of thinking. It is the first step in getting you where you want and need to go.

It is my prayer that you will not rush through this process. You will be laying the tracks your Train will travel along. These foundational rails will lead you on a journey to a world that only a few are willing to traverse. Permit yourself to enjoy the trip, understanding you may shed a few tears along the way. I applaud you in advance and wish you well as you take this ride to self-discovery.

Take time to make some notes on what has been presented so far before moving to the next chapter. All Aboard! in chapter 3, we will discover your "WHY."

NOTES:

"Your Soul Has A Beautiful Light Inside It, Don't Ever Dim It For Anyone."

– QuoteMamtra.com

SOUL SEARCHING USING THE TAPIN METHOD

"Discovering my "WHY" gave me motivation—knowing my "WHY" keeps me pushing forward when I feel like quitting. It made me UNSTOPPABLE!"

-Brenda Warren

Chapter 3

The Seven Why's

"Your willingness to learn and make adjustments when required will determine your ability to succeed." -Brenda Warren

The "Seven Why's" is a technique developed by Kurt Greening. The method is more commonly known as the Five Whys. Sackichi Toyota created them to get to the root cause of a problem. You start with the challenge. Keep asking "why?" until you have reached the point where you cannot go any further, or you found the limiting belief. You do not have to ask why seven times necessarily; just keep going until you reach your ending point.

When you discover your reason for wanting to make a change in your life, you can begin to make your transformation. Do you know why you want to make a change?

Many Travelers say they want to live a well-balanced life yet have trouble doing what is required to make that happen. Knowing your "why" proposition is key to lasting change.

Here is how you would work through this exercise:

We will start with ... **What is important to me about taking a trip to Grandma's House?** I will teach you soul searching using the TAPIN Method by taking an imaginary trip to Grandma's house.

1. Why is it important to teach soul searching and the TAPIN Method? *So that I can teach people to live a well-balanced life.*

2. Why do I want to teach people to live a well-balanced life? *So that they can have better outcomes in all areas of their lives.*

3. Why do I want people to have better outcomes? *I know what it is like to live an unbalanced life and not know what to do to change it.*

4. Why do I want people to change their Life? *So that they can have a better experience.*

5. Why do I want people to have a better experience? *Because you only get one Life to live! What a gift to be able to enjoy your Life thoroughly. I believe Life is too short to live in the negative.*

6. Why should people live the Life they enjoy? *They will have no regrets.*

7. Why should people have no regrets? *So that when life ends, they have had a full and happy life.*

I used all seven "Why's" for the above exercise. You may not think you have seven (7) why's, but keep trying and dig deep. The key is to work through the process to the end. I remember using twenty Why's when I became stuck on a particularly challenging area in my own life. Please, note seven would have been more than enough if I had been willing to be open and honest with myself. Keeping it real will save you lots of time and effort.

"The ship that you are waiting for to come in, may very well be the ship that you need to build." -Eddie Harris Jr

I always wanted to write about my Soul Searching and TAPIN Method. Fear kept me from putting pen to paper. Over the past few months, I reevaluated my concerns as I have begun to soul search even more profoundly, using my very own TAPIN Method to live my best life, becoming unapologetically unstoppable. I am now a Television Host, Podcaster, and an International Interviewer/Speaker, Course Creator, and published Bestselling Author as you are reading this book. All possible due to Soul Searching and the TAPIN Method. You can use the Seven Why's anytime you reach a stuck point in your life.

Use the previous example as your guide. Complete the Seven Why's, writing your questions and answers on the lines provided or in your journal before addressing the Core Beliefs Exercise in Chapter 4.

Make sure each question includes "why is" and the word "Important." Like "why is writing so important to you?" the answer is, "Because it allows me to express myself." You answer to the seventh time to find your why.

Why is _____ Important?
Because
Why is _____ Important?
Because
Why is _____ Important?
Because
Why is _____ Important?
Because
Why is _____ Important?
Because
Why is _____ Important?
Because
Why is _____ Important?
Because

Now that you have your why, we will use it as leverage to complete the core belief exercise in the next chapter.

NOTES:

"The Stronger The Why, The Easier The How Becomes."

– Jim Rohn

Chapter 4

Travelers' Core Beliefs

> *"Serving others is a way to fuel your spirit. It is a reminder you are a part of a community and not alone."*
> *– Brenda Warren*

I have always loved that quote. You can never go wrong by being of service and adding value. It is one of my core beliefs. What are your core beliefs? As a Traveler exploring your beliefs through soul searching, not knowing what you believe can be a little daunting. Your soul search exercise is essential to how you see yourself, others, and the future. Travelers' core beliefs become activated at each Platform. Example: A Traveler must challenge their thinking in most situations to successfully navigate this journey.

Your core beliefs get formed over time, through your experiences, and by believing what other people tell us to be true. Misinformation can and will taint core beliefs if allowed. I grew up in an environment that perpetuated the notion girls should be seen and not heard. It would take years for me to revoke that core belief and find my voice. Now it is one of my missions in life to be a voice for the voiceless and help them find their own.

Each Traveler entered the world an empty vessel. Our sterile containers would fill as we navigated our way through life. Some of the things poured into us would take a lifetime to remove. As children, we developed most of our core beliefs based on our parents and surroundings. I have now outgrown many of the core beliefs I had as a child.

You see, growing up in the projects, I had core beliefs about lack, poverty, and abundance. One of my opinions was that only certain people could have wealth. This followed me well into adulthood, although I was an entrepreneur at the age of nine. As I matured in life, I challenged my core beliefs about Religion, Money, Health, Relationships, and Business. I am saddened to say some have only changed in the last few years. My ability to pivot to a new way of thinking through Soul Searching using the TAPIN Method has done wonders to create balance in my life. It has allowed me to truly live unapologetically unstoppable. Discovering one's core beliefs can be separate training all by itself. Travelers need only focus on a few for this Soul Searching using The TAPIN Method. Although, I would encourage each Traveler dealing with trauma to do a detailed core belief review with a trained coach or licensed professional later.

Let us direct our attention to the Platforms we may land on, with two necessary additions ***Integrity*** and ***Respect for Others.*** They are significant drivers for how Travelers journey throughout life. Travelers with deficits in these two areas often find soul searching (and most other life tasks) a bit tricky. Take a moment to review the questions. Get clear on your core beliefs before beginning your soul searching exercise. Write out what are your core beliefs regarding:

Integrity – Are you worthy of trust? Do you keep your promises?

_____

_____

_____

_____

_____

_____

Respect for Others – Are you inclusive and collaborative with individuals with diverse backgrounds and talents so they can contribute and grow in your community?

_____

_____

_____

_____

Spirituality – Do you respect your faith and the right to others to believe what they choose?

_____

_____

_____

_____

Mental Health – Do you believe you can love yourself and still be a work in progress?

_____

_____

_____

_____

Physical Health/Wellness – Do you believe healthy practices are vital to well-balanced living?

___

___

___

___

Relationships - Do you believe relationships should be a safe haven, not a battlefield?

___

___

___

___

Finances – Do you make sound financial decisions?

___

___

___

___

Professional Development – Are you passionate about becoming the unrivaled best in your field or endeavor?
_____
_____
_____

Entrepreneurship (Owner) – Do you provide a quality product or service that meets your customer's needs?
_____
_____
_____
_____

Entrepreneurship (I want to start a business) – Are you ready to start your business?
_____
_____
_____
_____

SOUL SEARCHING USING THE TAPIN METHOD

Veterans– Are you ready to embrace civilian life?
_____
_____
_____
_____
_____

Keep your answers from the core beliefs questions front and center as you work through the next exercise. Remember, there are no right or wrong answers. The Soul Searching Exercise is not a test or a "got you." Travelers are embarking on a journey of SELF DISCOVERY. Each Traveler will discover something different. What you do after your exploration is what will make your trip worthwhile. It's now time to do your soul search. Travel with me to your next stop.

WANTED

A LIFE WORTH LIVING
*Filled with Love   *Life as my authentic self
*Lots of Laughter   *One I Design Myself
SOUL SEARCHING

NOTES:

"Focus On Making Choices To Lead Your Life That Aligns With Your Core Values In The Most Purposeful Way Possible."

-Roy T Bennett

Chapter 5

Soul Searching Exercise

"Soul Searching is a journey to wholeness and is worth the trip."
– Brenda Warren

To begin your soul search, find a quiet place. Please get comfortable. If done correctly, you may be here for a while. Soul Searching is for you! Do not cheat yourself during this experience. Write as much or as little as you need. Be honest and do not hold back. Using your journal explore these questions:

What would your perfect day look like?

What is the one thing you cannot live without?

What in life do you value the most?

What anxiety from your past, if any, affect you now?

What matters most, money, recognition, or free time?

What do you live for?

What is something you are proud of yourself for?

What do you need to forgive yourself for?

What are you judging yourself the hardest about?

How would people describe you?

What do you wish people knew about you?

Can you be 100% your authentic self?

What advice would you give your younger self?

What are your goals for the next 90 days?

What are your goals for the next six months?

What are your goals for the next year?

What do you want for yourself?

Who is most important to you?

Who is your role model? Why?

If money was no object, what would you be doing?

Describe your life Moto?

Are your current behaviors in line with that Moto?

What areas of my life need healing?

If the list did not include a question(s) vital to your journey, ask it before moving ahead. Be sure to write each question(s) and answer(s). Refer to the combined list as you do your soul search exercise.

<u>Using what you discovered from the questions you answered above, ponder the following:</u>

Take inventory. What do you really want...?

_____

_____

_____

_____

_____

Ask for guidance through prayer or meditation…
(www.prayer.com/www.calm.com)

_____

_____

_____

_____

Reflect on what is working well in your life…

_____

_____

_____

_____

Reflect on what is not working so well in your life…

_____

_____

_____

_____

Evaluate the support systems you have in place…

_____

_____

_____

_____

Determine if you are willing to explore holistic healing practices...
_____
_____
_____
_____

Are you willing to listen to the spirit inside of yourself...?
_____
_____
_____
_____

Do you want to be an Entrepreneur...?
_____
_____
_____
_____

If you are a Veteran, are you willing to get help and seek out resources...?
_____
_____
_____
_____

I wanted you to use this soul searching exploration and tap into the core of who you are. This information will enable you to move beyond the surface to find that part of yourself supplied with unlimited power for any endeavor. Soul searching is not about religious belief. It is about the universal law of purpose. When we let go of our limiting beliefs, anything is possible. Travelers, your soul searching results are your ticket to get clear about what you want. You can use the steps you have just learned to build a pattern for living. This process will enable you to create a well-balanced, unapologetically unstoppable life that you can enjoy.

Before you move into the TAPIN method section, I want you to be clear on how you want your life to look and feel. Knowing what you want will allow you to TAPIN heading in the direction of your desired outcome.

On the following few pages, you will record which areas of your life are off track, on track, or in need of adjustment. The soul search should have helped you determine what areas need realignment to live your best life. As a reminder, you get to choose which areas need attention. The most important thing is to be honest with yourself. This TAPIN is your journey, so enjoy the ride.

As you head toward the final stops of your soul search, take time to applaud yourself for what you have already accomplished. Congratulations on making it this far. Soul searching is not an easy process. Some people will never take the time to soul search. I have shed many tears as I worked through the very questions I placed before you. I continue to regularly address this book's thoughts for my own life. Life is continually changing. I am a work in progress, and I feel it is imperative to self-evaluate. Soul searching has allowed me to live the life I truly desire.

Soul Search Assignment:

It is time to use what you have uncovered. Use the lines provided below, a separate journal or on an electronic capture device to gain clarity. Indicate if you are on or off the track in the areas listed below.

Spiritual:

Mental:

Physical:

Relationship:

Financial:

Professional:

Entrepreneurship:

Veteran Services:

"When you do not control what you do, other people will control what you do."
-Brenda Warren

Connect With Yourself:

Take a moment to connect with yourself. How are you feeling about what you have uncovered so far? It can be overwhelming when you look inward. Permit yourself to write the story you want to live. I always say, "You have the pen, so why not make it an epic adventure?" Having a healthy relationship with yourself will require regular visits and demand time to process your emotions.

NOTES:

"My Life Is My Masterpiece, And I Reserve The Right To Make Changes As I See Fit."

-LaTisha Cotto

Off Track How Will You Get In Balance?

To continue please write at least one page in your Journal expressing your thoughts about each of the areas you have listed as off track. You should be specific about what is causing the imbalance. If only minor adjustments are needed, make them. For some Travelers, your trip can pause here; you have what you need for now. You can refer to the TAPIN Method in Chapter Six as required. You are already balanced, or in a position, you feel comfortable with where you are headed. Use the list below to notate how you plan to stay in balance in each area:

Spiritual: _____

Mental: _____

Physical: _____

Relationship: _____

Financial: _____

Professional: _____

Entrepreneurship: _____

Veteran Services: _____

"Doing "it" afraid is the gift I give myself."
-Brenda Warren

Dream Big!

You are now prepared to pick your TAPIN area(s). Take a moment to reflect on what you have uncovered so far. You will need to let go of limiting beliefs to truly benefit from the TAPIN Method. Your continuing Transformation is pages away. I want you to dream big and then dream bigger than that. Life is not a dress rehearsal. We only get one shot at this thing called life. You have the power to design a life you want to live and live it full out if you choose to. This time next year, how will your life appear? The choices you make from now on will be the reality you live in the future. Choose wisely.

NOTES:

_____

_____

_____

_____

_____

_____

_____

"Dream Big! And then dream bigger than that! Time to remove the limits."

-Brenda Warren

Remember This Is Your Journey!

Travelers in need of a practical set of guides to continue the journey to a well-balanced, unapologetically unstoppable life, please continue. Remember, this overall journey is about consistency over time, not perfection. Choose your TAPIN area(s). Which area(s) below will you use the TAPIN Method to address your current challenges?

Spiritual: _____

Mental: _____

Physical: _____

Relationship: _____

Financial: _____

Professional: _____

Entrepreneurship: _____

Veteran Services: _____

"While doing the soul search, you get to write your life's story. Make it one worth reading."
-Brenda Warren

Soul Searching Wrap Up:

Your first soul search is now complete. It would be best to determine how often you assess the state of your soul to ensure you remain unapologetically unstoppable. How you address negative and positive encounters will impact your ability to keep your soul flourishing.

Write out your thoughts in the note section below or a separate journal. You want to be clear as you enter the next phase of this journey.

Travelers in need of a breakdown, you are in luck! Are you ready to TAPIN? I will give you samples of the TAPIN Method for the eight most requested support areas. The journey to Grandma's continues in the next section.

NOTES:

TAPIN BONUS – AFFIRMATIONS

Affirmations are a part of my daily practice. You may already be familiar with the power of affirmations. They're short, positive statements that you can read, repeat to yourself, or listen to from recordings. With affirmations, you can reprogram your thinking

An example of an affirmation is *"I am unapologetically unstoppable!"* I was apologizing for everything when I first uttered those words. Your subconscious mind will pick up on the statement. In time your behavior will change to match your new belief. It doesn't matter your current state. The positive reinforcement created when they are a part of your daily routine may amaze you.

How To Use Affirmations

Concentrate on the things you want to change in your life. Try to keep it simple by focusing on one at a time.

Take time to develop affirmations for each area you choose to TAPIN. If you wrote one for wellness or mental fitness, you might use *"I feel energized"* or *"I bring positivity everywhere I go."* These are two of my personal favorites. Then choose a time to repeat the sayings to yourself every day. You can even make a recording of yourself repeating the affirmations with soothing music in the background. Recording them for playback is helpful and creates a solid link to your subconscious when you listen routinely.

Tips for writing your own affirmations:

- Write them in the present tense because that's the only way to improve your life in the present moment.
- Be short to keep things simple.
- Read and write your affirmations when you're calm and away from distractions.
- Remember to stay positive.

I have added some throughout the book if you do not want to write your own. Look online for additional ideas.

Affirmations For A Healthy Soul

- I determine the wellness of my soul based on my spiritual practices.

- When my soul flourishes, it helps me develop compassion for others in need.

- Being healthy, mind, body, and soul means I can live with a clear conscience.

- I train myself to let go of any negative energy in my life.

- I spend a few moments consciously opening my soul to positivity each morning.

- When I allow goodness to fill my soul, it reflects in my thoughts, words, and actions.

- My soul yearns to be embraced with love from the special people surrounding me. I leave their presence feeling blessed. I am sure to spend quality time with them daily.

- When I eliminate ego from my consciousness, I can offer sincere help. I avoid looking at what others think of my outreach. I do what feels right within my soul.

- I appreciate the beauty of the world. The beauty inspires me to live unapologetically unstoppable. Being conscious of the wonder around me adds positive energy to my life.

- Today, I commit to nurturing my soul with good things. I encourage love within my consciousness to extend love to people around me. I know that feeding it with optimistic truths is the key to ensuring my life remains positive and unapologetically unstoppable.

NOTES:

"Discovering Your Soul Purpose Is Freedom. Living Your Soul Purpose is Happiness. Sharing Your Soul Purpose In The World Makes You A Healer."

-Rhys Thomas

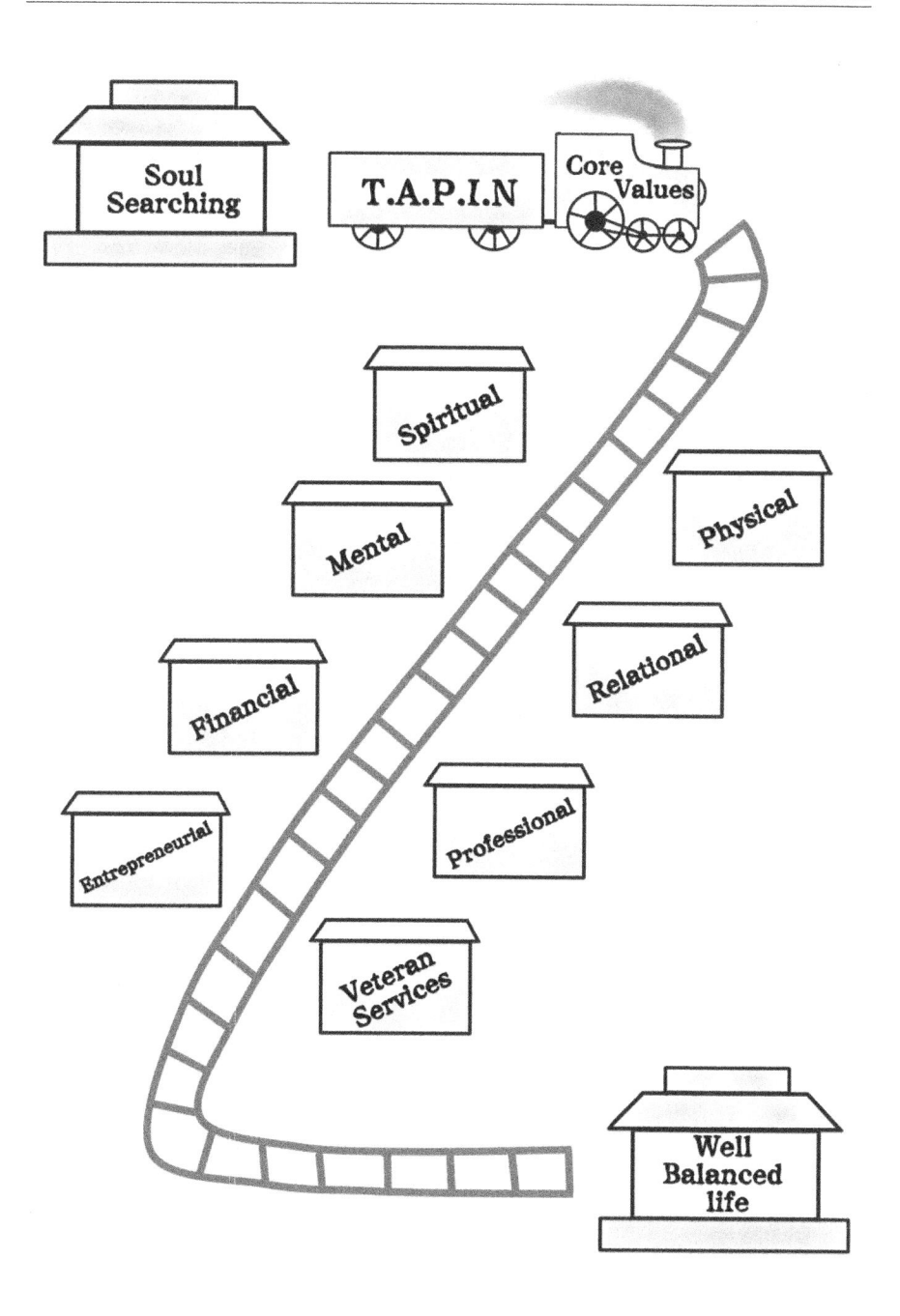

The TAPIN Method

Let's Jump The Track To The TAPIN Method

SECTION TWO

TAPIN Method

Chapter 6

What is TAPIN?

> *"You will never change a thing until you are ready to change a thing." – Brenda Warren*

The TAPIN Method was created when I needed a straightforward way to assist my Travelers, in making positive changes in their lives without switching systems. I am a firm believer that life is not one size fits all. We are all designers'; originals worthy of programs tailored to our specific needs and desires. I prided myself in providing individualized plans suited for each of the unique souls entrusted to my care. How would I customize my process, yet still keep it flexible enough to help those struggling with living a well-balanced, unapologetically unstoppable life? My additional mandate of helping the voiceless find their voice made this a thought-provoking process.

I started by taking inventory of what were the everyday struggles I was recruited to solve. Many a tired soul reported feeling out of balance:

Spiritually – Lack of connection, no answers to burning questions, and disillusionment with current religious practice.

Mentally – Brain fog, blahs, no direction, depression (sent to professional);

Physically – Overweight, lack of exercise and no motivation.

Relationally – Poor communication, infidelity, lack of sex drive, and relationship roles.

Financially - Debt management.

Professionally – Professional development and lack of growth in the current career field.

Entrepreneurially – Burnout/Business startup.

Veterans Services – Post-traumatic Stress Disorder (PTSD), Military Sexual Trauma (MST) and adjusting to civilian life.

Many Travelers indicated that they felt unable or unwilling to speak what was, indeed, on their minds. These eight life issues and my Travelers' inability to speak their truths became my targets of focus. Yes, there were even more areas; however, these eight showed up without fail.

I needed a transformational tool that was easy to navigate. One that could translate regardless of the area of change we traversed. Some of the people I coached, consulted, and mentored had a different method for every area of their life in need of course correction. I developed the TAPIN Method to combine with Soul Searching to provide a customizable system universal in each of the identified problem areas and beyond.

The beauty of TAPIN is that you are given, a system that will cross the tracks while keeping you on course to reach your desired destination. The TAPIN Method allows you to take temporary departures as needed. Need to go sightseeing? Feel free and get right back on track for success when you are ready. TAPIN will not derail if you choose to disembark at any point along your journey as long as you get back on board.

This five-step strategic process will be integral to getting you to your desired destination of spiritual, mental, physical, relational, financial, professional, and entrepreneurial wholeness. If you are a Veteran TAPIN can help with managing the stress of PTSD/MST. It is a valuable supplement to your professional counseling when properly utilized. It can help with your travels through the civilian world. Veterans must get clear on what is essential during their transition. Using the resources at the end of the book can help you with this process. This program will give you the confidence to lift your voice and speak your truth. Travelers can use the TAPIN Method as your foundation for a well-balanced, unapologetically unstoppable life. It is a pattern for living and is designed to help you create a soul searching trip worth taking. Travelers have reported using TAPIN to establish cleaning routines, savings plans, study habits and more. The TAPIN Method is a simple yet powerful way of targeted soul searching to get to what you want. Your imagination only limits your options for using the TAPIN Method.

TAPIN is an acronym for:

T- Transformation - Tell yourself something good to transform your mind

A – Announcement/Accountability – Announce YOUR intentions and be accountable

P - Preparation - Prepare for your desired outcome

I – Imagination – Visualize you are already in possession of your desired change

N – Nurture – Cultivate your dream

In the upcoming pages, continuing with our train theme from previous chapters, Travelers will be guided on applying each step in the TAPIN Method as they read along. TAPIN Platforms are solid landings to create the change or adjustments you need on your trip. The platforms you choose will determine which area of your life you will be addressing. Only adjust as required. You may be whole in some regions. Applying the TAPIN Method as needed, you can help balance each area of your life. Remember, this is ***YOUR JOURNEY***; you get to plan this adventure. You get to decide how many platforms you travel to for this trip. The TAPIN Method will be your map to place you on the right track to your new pattern for living. They say the journey of a thousand miles starts with the first step. Step on board, and let us take this trip to wholeness together.

NOTES:

"Your Daily Habits Will Determine Your Outcomes."

-Brenda Warren

AFFIRMATIONS

When it comes to the world of affirmations, the only requirement is to approach it with an open mind. After that, you simply allow the statements to wash over you and you can change your life all by yourself.

It may seem difficult at first, but the key is to get the affirmation into your subconscious mind. This is easiest when you're just waking up or when you're drifting off to sleep. These are moments when your conscious mind is less likely to interfere. Chose a few from the list below or write your own:

- I am ready to TAPIN to my greatness
- I know what I want out of life
- I keep my desires at the top of my mind every day
- I soul search regularly
- I am prepared to do whatever it takes to make my dreams come true
- I let go of things that no longer serve me
- I keep an open mind
- I am prepared to deal with whatever comes my way
- Positive affirmations help me focus on my goals.
- I believe I can achieve the goals I set for myself
- Positive affirmations help keep me focused and at the top of my game.

Believing you can change is the first step in any transformation. The second is taking action to get the results you desire. Be consistent and align your behaviors to your beliefs.

-Brenda Warren

Chapter 7
TAPIN

TRANSFORMATION - Tell Yourself Something Good to Transform Your Mind

> *" When you change your beliefs, you change your behavior. Consistency over time is critical to transformation."*
> *- Brenda Warren*

What you tell yourself matters. Every day we are bombarded with useless information that serves us no purpose. Combined with the subconscious stories that play in our heads over and over again like broken records. We must learn to control our thoughts, or our limiting beliefs will keep us held hostage.

Nothing is more powerful than the things you tell yourself. What did you think when I asked you to join me on a trip to my Grandma's House? If you told yourself you could not go, you could not afford it, or any other reason, your brain automatically ensured that you would not. The opposite is true, as well. When you make up your mind that you can accomplish a task, your mind will guide you in that direction

Your mindset is the key to unlocking the power inside yourself. I spent years not accomplishing what I said I desired the most due to "stinking thinking" and limiting beliefs. I listened to the lies I told myself about my weight, gender, finances, voice, and worthiness. I am no longer bound by those distractive voices in my head that told me I could never.

What is your "I could never?" Grab your journal; explore for a moment the negative things you tell yourself. List the things that continue to hold you back from living your best life. I do not want you to spend too much time there. I just need you to acknowledge the beliefs that have you stuck. The Seven Why's is always useful when stuck (refer to chapter 3). Once you have identified them, you will replace them with empowering beliefs to travel on a more fulfilled life path.

I believe that "I AM" statements are the most powerful creative force statements on the planet. When we declare, "I am," the universe wakes up to make it happen. You may have heard; Life and death are in the power of the tongue. The words you speak over your life will indeed determine how far you go on your journey.

Travelers that continually speak negative words surrounding their circumstances will find themselves stranded in the train stations of life. Travelers taking a more positive approach can be found traveling around the world or to the next town with a smile. They are full of hope and can see the positive, even on rainy days. You know, the ones that are always saying things like:

Positive Self Talk Traveler	**Negative Self Talk Traveler**
I deserve love and respect as I am	No one will ever love me
I am a person that sometimes fails	I am a failure
I am thankful for what my body is capable of; I am healthy and fit	I hate my body and how it looks. I will always be fat

I cannot begin to express the importance of what you tell yourself. Travelers, I encourage you to speak life over yourself, or your trip could be over even before it gets started. I have watched more travelers talk themselves out of successful journeys than I care to tell you.

As I travel my own journey, I tell myself only the positive things that will allow me to live my best experience. I repeatedly tell myself I am fit, fierce, and fabulous. I tell myself I am out of debt, and all my needs are met; Money is coming all the time. I tell myself my voice matters, and I only use it to inspire. I tell myself there is nothing I cannot do.

Lisa Nichols' "Mirror Work Exercise" has been instrumental in what I tell myself. This life-changing exercise revolutionized how I see myself. Watch "Why Mirror Work Will Change Your Life – Lisa Nichols," on YouTube for a mind-blowing experience. Daily I stood in the mirror and told myself seven things in three different categories. I did this during the Speak to Inspire Quest presented by Mind Valley, www.mindvalley.com. Over thirty days, I shed a lot of tears and gained great healing. It is a practice I continue daily. Here is how you can do it:

TELL YOURSELF

Write out 7 things that you are PROUD of yourself for, speak them to yourself out loud while standing in front of the mirror:

1. _____

2. _____

3. _____

4. _____

5. _____

6. _____

7. _____

CELEBRATE YOU!

Write out 7 things that you FORGIVE yourself for, speak them to yourself out loud while standing in front of the mirror:

1. _____

2. _____

3. _____

4. _____

5. _____

6. _____

7. _____

The journey to self-forgiveness is not always comfortable. It will take time and much self-reflection. I heard recently; life does not happen to us; it happens for us. Remind yourself you made the best decision(s) you knew how and permit yourself to let "it" go.

FORGIVE YOURSELF!

Write out 7 things that you COMMIT to yourself, speak them to yourself out loud while standing in front of the mirror:

1. _____

2. _____

3. _____

4. _____

5. _____

6. _____

7. _____

My life, I heard the term, "Your word is your bond." I have not always kept my word to myself. The truth is, I have kept the negative stories that have held me hostage. The "I can't's," etc. Decide to keep the commitments you make to yourself. Begin to honor your words and make them life-affirming and joyous.

HONOR YOU!

What are you telling yourself?

Tell yourself what you want. Take the limits off what is possible, allowing yourself to state your most pressing desire freely. I want you to dream big! Then dream bigger than that. The how you get there is figured out along the way. On the Transformation seat, you change your mindset.

What are you telling yourself regularly?

_____

_____

_____

_____

_____

_____

_____

_____

_____

_____

_____

_____

_____

_____

I AM AFFIRMATIONS

These are some of the "I Am" Affirmations I use daily:

I Am ENOUGH

I Am Worthy

I Am Loved

I Am Capable

I Am Strong

I Am Fit

I Am Fierce

I Am Fabulous

Write your own I Am statements below:

I Am _____

I Am _____

I Am _____

I Am _____

I Am _____

I Am _____

I Am _____

I Am _____

NOTES:

"What You Say To Yourself Matters! Tell Yourself Something Good. Your Healthy Mental Health Depends On It."

-Brenda Warren

Chapter 8
TAPIN

Announcement and Accountability – Announce YOUR Intentions and Be Accountable

> *"Tell me about your daily routine, and I can tell you about your future."*
> *- Brenda Warren*

Making an explicit declaration of your intention is one way to show the world you mean business. I have decided to take a trip to Grandma's House by Train. Now you have decided to join me. When do we plan to take this trip, and what will be required?

The key to your intentions is to be as specific as possible. Be sure you are crystal clear, so there is no room for misunderstanding. Announcing your purposes is not just for you. It is about creating accountability. Studies show people are more likely to complete the project, even personal ones when there is some form of responsibility involved.

Announcing your intentions is critical in establishing your goals or making plans to change the areas of concern. Clarifying what you want and making a bold declaration will ensure you are heading in the right direction. Adding an accountability component will take you to the next level.

Issuing and preparing your statements of intentions to be unapologetically unstoppable in the area(s) of the TAPIN you have decided to work on is crucial to seeing it through. Making a definite decision in writing and speaking it aloud will get you headed down the right track.

Make The Announcement

What are YOUR intentions for your Life?

_____

_____

_____

_____

_____

_____

Become Accountable

While attending the ***Be On TV Challenge***, one of the first assignments instructed me to get an accountability buddy. Mine arrived in the form of a fellow veteran named Lisa Ducharme. Lisa's no-nonsense approach to accountability was just what I needed. Also, Lisa, an Air Force Veteran of over 20 years, was unwilling to give me a pass. She said, "suck it up!" when I fell into the woe is me mode.

The truth is, I was terrified at the thought of having to be accountable to someone. Looking back, I now understand how I have remained stuck in so many areas of my life. My lack of accountability allowed me to live in the shadows. I provided a space for myself to do a lot while accomplishing the very minimum. Being accountable has allowed me to grow in ways that I don't have enough book space or time to express.

The best part is that my accountability partner is a straight shooter. I will be told the truth even when I don't want to hear it. Are you willing to be held accountable? Who in your current circle would you trust to hold you responsible?

Make a list of the area(s) you require accountability. Write in your journal or in the space provided below:

Areas requiring accountability:

_____

_____

_____

_____

_____

_____

Make a list of possible accountability buddies:

_____

_____

_____

_____

_____

_____

You are starting to pick up momentum. Stay on track! Announcing your intentions and getting an accountability partner are essential to living your dreams. Becoming unapologetically unstoppable started with your mindset shift. Here in the Announcement /Accountability seat, you declare your intended change, you say it aloud, and take responsibility!

NOTES:

"Accountability Is The Glue That Ties Comment To Results."

- Bob Proctor

Chapter 9
TA**P**IN

Preparation - Prepare For Your Desired Outcome

> *"Those who stay prepared will always be prepared for any opportunity as it is presented."*
> *-Brenda Warren*

Preparation is a clear indication you are expecting something to happen. With our trip decided, date and time set, mode of transportation in place, we have a starting point for our adventure. Preparation in this stage of the TAPIN Method is vital to ensure we travel the tracks with ease. Whatever area(s) you are looking to make adjustments in, you will need to prepare. We would need to purchase tickets for our train trip to see Grandma. We may even need to get rides to the train station pack our luggage; you get the idea. With no preparation, our trip would have already stalled.

Your trip has started, and along the way, you may notice the train is a little chilly and might need to stop to purchase a sweater. You may see you are not happy with the other riders on your current train. Switching train cars is not always a comfortable process. Sometimes a different train car may be easier to enjoy. Whatever you do, don't stop your trip; simply take a break.

I have three Guinea Pigs; S'Mores, a boy; River and Misty, both girls. They are my service pets. These beautiful little souls take lots of care to maintain. I must plan for their daily maintenance to ensure they are fed, cleaned, and loved. It is like having three infants, as they require constant care. Preparation ensures I have enough hay, spring water, bedding, and veggies to keep them happy. Without proper care, a Guinea Pig's system can shut down in about twelve hours. They are not pocket pets and require exotic veterinarian care to maintain appropriate health care. It takes an enormous amount of preparation to care for my piggies.

What preparations are needed to make your intentions come to pass? What are you willing to do to prepare for what you say matters to you? List it in your journal or write it on the lines below:

What do I need to be prepared for?

_____

_____

_____

_____

_____

_____

_____

_____

In the Preparation seat, you plan for your desired outcome. Using a SMART Goals format, Travelers get on track with ease:

S - Get *"Specific."* Describe your goal in detail.

M - They are" *Measurable."* How will you track your progress?

A - Take *"Action."* What three steps can you take to reach your goal?

R - Make it *"Relevant."* Why is this goal important to you?

T - Must be *"Time Bound."* When will you reach your goal?

Sample of SMART Goals I used:

Specific:

I will lose thirty (30) pounds by the end of 2022. Additionally, I plan to weight train and gain flexibility in the process during my daily exercise.

Measurable:

I will conduct weekly weigh-ins and tape measure myself to check my progress. I will have lost all thirty (30) pounds by December 2022.

Action:

With my Physicians support, I will exercise seven days a week. Two days outdoors Five days in my home gym. I will walk within my limitations. I will use a combination of free weights and videos. I will report my results to my accountability buddy. I will change my eating habits to allow this process to happen steadily over time.

Relevant:

This lifestyle change will help me TAPIN to my continued wellness plan and be in line with what I have been teaching for years.

Time-Bound:

I will have this process completed by December 2022. Creating a lifestyle, I can maintain.

"I believe everyone has a story (weight loss etc..). I love to write stories because I get to choose the ending. Now I am writing the story I Want To Live. Will you write yours?"
-Brenda Warren

SMART Goal Listing to get you started on the right track:

Specific:
_____
_____
_____

Measurable:
_____
_____
_____

Action:
_____
_____
_____

Relevant:
_____
_____
_____

Time-Bound:
_____
_____
_____

Practice setting SMART Goals for yourself in your journal.

NOTES:

"People With Goals Succeed Because They Know Where They Are Going."

-Earl Nightingale

"Imagination is the playground that fuels your soul."

-Brenda Warren

Chapter 10
TAPIn

Imagination - Visualize You Are Already in Possession of Your Change

> *"Your Imagination is the limitless well only you can let run dry."*
> *-Brenda Warren*

Imagination is a gift given to man by his Creator. Visualization allows you to see yourself already at your desired place. Although you have not been to Grandma's house, I can assure you that sweet potato pies and chocolate-covered bacon will be waiting when we arrive. A trip to the farmer's market for fried shrimp, crab legs and Dutch Country Cheese will soon follow. No trip to my hometown would be complete without a trip to the hoagie shop for an Italian hoagie (sub) fully loaded and a Philly Cheesesteak. Can you smell the aroma of all the foods listed? Placing yourself at the center of your desired outcome is one way to keep you on track.

The creative power of the human mind is so mighty. Athletes and professionals alike use visualization to train for their events. When you get a clear picture of your desired outcome in your mind, it has to come to pass. I believe people can achieve whatever they conceive.

In the Imagination seat, you will use your imagination and visualize yourself already in possession of your desired outcome. However, if you are not, think of your wish to be spiritually, mentally, and physically changed or different. Imagine what it would look like. Want a better job? Imagine what it would be. Want to be an Entrepreneur?

I want you to plan your grand opening. No matter where your travels take you, I want you to imagine yourself already there.

I have always had a great imagination. As a child, I was often admonished to get my head out of the clouds. I created worlds in my head that would help me escape to safety. As an adult, my ability to visualize helped me see past the fear that held me drowning in plain sight. This same book you are now reading was first envisioned right down to the book release. In fact, the book cover for the first edition was created before a word was ever written.

In your journal or on the lines below, I would like you to write out a detailed story describing your desires as if they have already manifested.

What have you imagined for your life?

_____

_____

_____

_____

_____

_____

_____

_____

YOUR DREAMS are only limited by your imagination. I want you to visualize living your dreams without apology. Imagine yourself living a well-balanced, unapologetically unstoppable life in the Imagination seat. One you may have only dreamed of having. Take a trip through your imagination and visualize what you want. Do not focus on the how. Let your imagination soar! In your journal or on the lines that follow, get on track with the thing that is your passion:

What would your perfect well-balanced, unapologetically unstoppable life look like to you?

_____
_____
_____
_____
_____
_____
_____
_____
_____
_____
_____
_____
_____
_____
_____
_____

TAPIN TIPS

Need additional help visualizing your dreams? Check out "Create Your Story With A Vision Board," in the bonus section at the back of the book.

NOTES:

"IMAGINATION Should Be Used, Not To Escape Reality But To Create It."

- Colin Wilson

Chapter 11
TAPI**N**

Nurture – Cultivate Your Dream

> *"I Dreamed big! Then I dreamed bigger than that, once I realized I could write the dream I want to live."*
> *-Brenda Warren*

Nurturing your dreams is key to making them grow. When our innermost desires are held in high esteem, we will move heaven and earth to make them a reality. Nurturing your dream is the final and one of the most critical steps of this process. The ability to see your vision is the only way to ensure it becomes a reality. You and I would have arrived at Grandma's House by now. She has gathered all the family, and they are so happy to see us both. Sitting on the porch, we can look back at all it took to get us to this point. Now that we've figured out how to get here, we can use this same process to go anywhere else we choose to travel. The next chapter will get you started traveling on your TAPIN journey in the direction towards spiritual, mental, physical, relational, financial, professional, and entrepreneurial freedom. Veterans will find a whole chapter of resources at the end.

One of my many dreams was to be a writer. I was always a great talker, but I wanted to put pen to paper. Being grammatically challenged made this seem like an impossible task. I would write in secret for years, afraid and not wanting to be laughed at. I was eventually asked to write an article. It was rejected. I never asked why it was not used. I was too traumatized to investigate. I simply believed I was not good enough, so I never tried again. During the Be On TV Challenge, I was required to write and speak aloud, on video, the things I had written. Those exercises gave me the courage to write this book.

In your journal or on the lines below, write out some of the dreams you would like to manifest:

What are some dreams you have held in secret?

_____

_____

_____

_____

_____

_____

In the Nurture seat, you will cultivate your dreams. What dream has laid dormant due to self-imposed limiting beliefs? It is time to take them out of that boxcar, so your dreams can travel the world. In your journal or on the lines below, share a vision you would like to fast track to your future:

How can you nurture the dreams you have for yourself?

_____

_____

_____

_____

_____

_____

NOTES:

"The Biggest Adventure You Can Take Is To Live The Life Of Your Dreams."

- Oprah Winfrey

Chapter 12

How to Apply TAPIN to your Life

> *"The decisions you make today will be the reality you live tomorrow. Choose wisely."* –Brenda Warren

This section will give you a few examples used by previous Travelers' to TAPIN into specific areas. These are not hard and fast. They are meant as guide rails to get you started down the tracks toward your destination. Remember, this is your journey. You must plan the trip you want to take. Each Platform is a landing space for you to design the stop you need before moving on to the next. The Platform you start on is determined by you. However, I would like to suggest your first time through do your TAPIN in the order listed. This has proven to be the most successful

Some travelers will board the train, stopping at one Platform at a time. Adventurous Travelers will make multiple stops, jumping from one Platform to the next with ease. You may even want to go around the track several times and visit platforms repeatedly. Regardless of how you personally choose to travel, please enjoy your trip. The key to a good journey is always in the planning. When you fail to plan, you plan to fail.

Choosing your first platform is the next order of business. When selecting the order of your Platforms, I encourage you to start with the Spiritual Platform first? The Spiritual Platform is the stop that will support all the other stops along the tracks. This is not about religion; it is about having a foundation. Once again, your core beliefs a paramount in establishing your journey boundaries. The other platforms can go in any order you choose.

Although the listing is not all-inclusive, I have identified the most common types of Travelers that I have encountered as I worked with different ones. All the platforms listed have been visited by each of the described Travelers with various outcomes. Each journey is unique. Only the Traveler designing their trip can determine the development of their particular journey.

There can be many platforms potentially your train could stop at. However, for the purpose of this book, I have chosen eight. Review the list below to decide where you would like to stop. You may change your mind about which platform to begin with after reading each Platform's sample TAPIN. That is ok, as changing platforms is an easy process. Remember to allow your core values engine to be the driving force:

- The Spiritual Platform is where you set your foundation. If you have no spiritual practice skip to the Platform of your choice.

- The Mental Health Platform is where you build your mindset and emotional health.

- The Physical Health and Wellness Platform is where you get in shape and build your health wealth.

- The Relationship Platform is where you evaluate how you view your relationships.

- The Financial Platform is where you build your money management skills.

- The Professional Platform is where you evaluate your career choices.

- The Entrepreneurship Platform is where you explore if business ownership is in your future.

- The Veteran Services Platform is where you explore transition and guide you toward resources. (also see chapter 16)

Take detailed notes in your journal as you work through your TAPIN. Each of the following sections contains sample TAPIN Quick Notes lines to give you a place for (you guessed it) quick notes. Additionally, sample TAPIN guides have been added as prompts. They are simply your road map for you to create your own TAPIN adventure at each platform as you journal your way through the process. You are designing your well-balanced, unapologetically unstoppable life as you land on each platform.

This Sample TAPIN Quick Notes will appear at the end of each section to remind you to TAPIN!

T	**Transformation**
A	**Announcement/Accountability**
P	**Preparation**
I	**Imagination**
N	**Nurture**

TAPIN Method PROMPT SAMPLES

T - sample actions you will take to move toward transformation

A - sample announcements and accountability

P - sample preparation action and steps

I - sample descriptions of intention

N - sample of how you will nurture you dream

TAPIN TIPS

Tips May Not Always Appear

Use The Tips That Seem Right To You

Tips Are Reminders This Is Your Journey

Use Your Journal It Is Great For Reflection

NOTES:

"Get Into The Habit Of Asking Yourself, Does This Support The Life I'm Trying To Create?"

- Jade Marie

Chapter 13

Sample TAPIN's

> *"Life is too short to live in the negative."* -Brenda Warren

1. The Spiritual Platform

Each Traveler's spiritual journey is unique. It is by far the most personal stage of this trip, in my view.

Regardless of your religious affiliation, your opinion of God, Universe, or Creator. The spiritual platform is essential to every trip you will ever take. Spirituality is usually a significant component that will be the foundation of your entire journey. How you set the groundwork for navigating this stage of your trip will forever change how you travel. Here you will gather strength as you decide what you believe. Additionally, your core beliefs are the engine that drives all future travel along a set of stable tracks.

My spiritual journey continues today as I take the limits off my beliefs and allow for the infinite possibilities I was born to inherit. I no longer place unrealistic limits on God. I have become open to all the endless gifts this life offers. I travel through this life attached to no one way to see God, free to enjoy his magnificence beyond what I can comprehend. My current life path leads me to believe He is sovereign. Also, I think I have no right to decide what others believe. My core beliefs will enable me to keep positive in a world not always conducive to my way of thinking.

If you have no core beliefs, you will have broken rails and loose ties at a minimum. Inconsistent beliefs can lead to accidents. If your core beliefs are not stable, your train can experience delays and detours. It could even derail without you being in fear. Knowing that your foundation is solid will help you travel smoothly from stop to stop, supported by well-installed tracks. Developing your foundational truth is paramount to maintaining your transformed habits.

Types of Travelers Boarding the Spiritual Platform

- Travelers at the end of their spiritual rope are often broken. No longer willing to take a trip with any religion.

- Platform-hopping Travelers that jump from one spiritual experience to another with no clear vision for their trip.

- Weary Travelers that have tried many religions, but were never really satisfied, are still soul searching.

- Commitment-ready Travelers ready and open to a lifelong commitment to good spiritual practice.

- Seasoned Travelers who have already been on their personal spiritual journey. They would not consider going on any trip without their faith.

- None of the above.

What is your Traveler type? What are your spiritual needs?

_____
_____
_____
_____
_____
_____

Whatever your current traveling style, here are a few samples for your TAPIN before you list your own:

Spiritual TAPIN METHOD SAMPLES

T - Daily practice of Bible study, religious reading, prayer, Yoga, or meditation

A - Profess your faith; get a partner to connect on a mobile app or social media group, join a congregation

P - Purchase study material, clear a study space, and schedule a time to study

I - Imagine yourself with an implemented spiritual practice that helps you fulfill your calling

N - Nurturing your spiritual practice is a lifestyle choice that will keep you grounded

Reminder below use your journal to begin your TAPIN:

T	**Transformation**
A	**Announcement/Accountability**
P	**Preparation**
I	**Imagination**
N	**Nurture**

TAPIN TIPS

Find What Works For You

Study For Yourself

Listen To Music That Bring You Joy

NOTES:

"Through Prayer And Meditation, I Create A Ripple Effect Of Peace In The World."

- Unknown

2. Mental Health Platform

Your mental health must become a priority. The stress of daily living makes the Mental Health Platform one you have to pay close attention to. Lack of sleep, combined with poor exercise habits, makes this a dangerous stop to avoid. When left unchecked, mental health can deteriorate rapidly and lead to significant setbacks.

In 2011 I was diagnosed with Post-traumatic Stress Syndrome (PTSD) and Military Sexual Trauma (MST). My shame and feeling of failure surrounding these diagnoses left me scared and alone. I feared telling my family, boss, co-workers, or peers. I did not want to lose my job as a Director at the hospital. The stress of maintaining this secret would lead to a complete mental breakdown that sent me into early retirement.

Looking back, I wish I had developed the TAPIN Method sooner to help me get on track at one of my life's darkest times. Instead, I was drowning in plain sight because I would not seek help. If you need help, there are counselors trained to assist you. Call your primary care physician, reach out to friends and family, or call 911. If you are in crisis, you can contact the national crisis hotline at 1-800-273-8255 (Veterans press 1). Confidential chat is available at VeteransCrisisLine.net or just send a text to 838255.

Every Tuesday, I make the "Tell Yourself Tuesday" post on all my social media platforms. I started them initially to help me deal with my mental health issues. They have become some of my most popular videos. I encourage every Traveler to find an activity that will help them improve their mental health. For my fellow Veterans or anyone diagnosed with Post-traumatic Stress Syndrome (PTSD), I would like to suggest a re-frame to help you get through your day, which helped me.

I learned reframing your thoughts does not mean changing an opposing view to a positive one. I had to switch to a realistic perspective. I reframed my opinions concerning the eight areas covered in TAPIN to reduce my stress and live a peaceful life. Additionally, it helped me think, feel, and act more rationally.

A simple reframing exercise I do when I find myself challenged by a negative emotional thought is to ask myself the following questions:

- What is the gift in this situation?
- How can I turn this situation into a positive?
- What is the best way to act in this situation?
- What if I choose to believe the opposite of how I feel?

By asking the right questions, it allowed me to reframe my thinking regarding PTSD or anything else that is bothering me. Reframing your thoughts is a vital component taught throughout TAPIN.

As I continued to deal with depression off and on, I had to learn "whys" to manage my daily life. My management tool was to reframe what PTSD meant to me. Now I simply "*Plan To Show Up Daily.*" It was a simple adjustment that has helped me get through some rough days. I work with Travelers to remove their limiting beliefs about mental health, always wanting to prevent another unnecessary silence.

Types of Travelers on the Mental Health Platform

- Travelers without a precise support system, not knowing were to get help.
- Travelers that are searching with no clear vision for their mental health needs.
- Weary Travelers that have tried many support groups.
- Travelers ready to commit to seeking professional help.
- Seasoned Travelers who are already adamant about their need to protect their mental health at all costs.
- None of the above.

What is your Traveler Type? What are your mental health care needs?

SOUL SEARCHING USING THE TAPIN METHOD

_____

_____

_____

You will want to practice self-care, developing a routine you will stick with, making it a lifestyle. Whatever your current traveling style, here are a few samples for your TAPIN before you list your own:

Mental Health TAPIN METHOD SAMPLES

T - Self-care, positive affirmation, work on your thought life, and exercise

A - Reach out to a safe support person or join a support group

P - Seek professional counseling if needed, study emotional intelligence

I - Imagine what a clear, healthy, positive mind would feel like

N - Create an environment that promotes healthy mental health practices

Reminder below use your journal to begin your TAPIN:

T	**Transformation**
A	**Announcement/Accountability**
P	**Preparation**
I	**Imagination**
N	**Nurture**

TAPIN TIP

Know Your Worth

NOTES:

I Became Unapologetically Unstoppable when I Realized I Didn't Need Someone Else's Permission To Unplug and Reevaluate. If I don't Take Care Of My Mental Health, No one Eles Will. The Guilt And Shame Are Gone. I Am Learning To Make Me A Priority."

- Brenda Warren

3. Physical Health and Wellness Platform

You only get one body. It seems silly to say that most Travelers treat their automobiles better than they treat their physical bodies. Cars are chosen with great care, often polished weekly, serviced monthly, and sent to detailers. Unfortunately, Travelers will barely keep dental or eye annual appointments.

I was one of those Travelers. Like many women, I told myself I could not lose my weight after having my child. I kept buying bigger and bigger clothes, resigned to the fact I would never again be able to wear the cute outfits that once filled my walk-in closet. Imagine my horror the day I stepped into the lady's dressing room, and the only thing that fit was a size twenty-six!

With two herniated discs in my lower back, I was told nothing could be done. Fibromyalgia and sciatica made the pain unbearable. I finally got tired of being told what I could not do and asked what *I could* do. I started with intermitted fasting. I fasted for sixteen hours a day and eat in an eight-hour eating window. I reduced my carbohydrate intake and cut out all snacks. I also did my research because health and fitness are not one size fits all. I had already been on every diet known to exist. None of them worked until I discovered my unique approach, geared just to my body and its specific needs. I encourage Travelers to be patient and to do their research to find out what will work for their bodies. A cookie-cutter program will never replace a customized plan. A plan you will develop geared to your individual needs.

After much trial and error, a few additional injuries and more weight gain, I started walking in my driveway 15 minutes at a time. Eventually, I walked every hour on the hour to pain tolerance daily until I reached 10,000 steps. It took all day. I hired a personal trainer after I lost 59 pounds on my own. My first workout was more challenging than I anticipated. I wanted to give up. Investing in getting healthy was so significant, and the benefit will be long-lasting. I now live a fasted focus lifestyle. I exercise daily to maintain my weight and reduce stress. These practices help to keep me in balance while ensuring my health wealth. #Noexcuses

Types of Travelers on the Physical Health and Wellness Platform

- Travelers unwilling to do the necessary work to get healthy.
- Travelers that have tried every fad diet and have given up all hope.
- Travelers that are Vegan, ones living a fasted focus lifestyle, maybe even Keto friendly.
- Weary Travelers that have tried many times to start an exercise program.
- Commitment-ready Travelers ready and open to a new fitness and wellness lifestyle.
- Seasoned Travelers already living a fitness and wellness lifestyle journey and would not consider living anything less.
- None of the above.

What is your Travel Type? What are your physical health and wellness needs?

_____

_____

_____

_____

_____

Whatever your current traveling style, here are a few samples for your TAPIN before you list your own:

Physical health and Wellness TAPIN METHOD SAMPLES

T - Decide how much weight you want to lose or, in some cases, want to gain

A - Post the number in plain sight and tell friends and family

P - Join a gym or purchase workout gear and equipment for a home workout

I - Imagine yourself at your goal weight or outfit

N - Develop a unique plan for yourself; eat healthily, exercise and treat yourself to non-food rewards

Reminder below use your journal to begin your TAPIN:

T	**Transformation**
A	**Announcement/Accountability**
P	**Preparation**
I	**Imagination**
N	**Nurture**

TAPIN TIPS

Do What Feels Good

Stop Workouts You Hate

Move In Ways That Bring You Joy

Eat What You Love, Eat Healthy

NOTES:

"Take Care Of Your Body. It's The Only Place You Have To Live."

- Jim Rohn

4. Relationships Platform

Abraham Maslow places "to love and to belong" dead center of his hierarchy of needs. We search for our purpose among our friends and family in love and belonging. Often using his example, people look for external validation before realizing happiness is an inside job. On this Platform, I challenge the Traveler to first work on Maslow's purported next need: self-esteem, which includes self-validation before looking outside of yourself.

As an avid life-long learner, I would be well into my fifties before discovering that loving myself would be needed before I could truly love another the way it was intended. The Relationship Platform is full of possibilities. This is a stop filled with many twists and turns contingent on how you choose to show up at this junction in your journey.

This platform will challenge Travelers in so many ways. With so many different types of relationships, you may decide to do a general TAPIN or break your TAPIN down as follows:

- Family - Mother, Father, Sister, Brother, Grandparents, Aunt, Uncle etc.,
- Friends - Best, Associates, Casual, Frenemy,
- Partners – Spouse, Ex-Spouse, Boyfriend, Girlfriend, Significant Other,
- Lovers – Past, Present, Future,
- Professional – Boss, Peers, Co-Workers, Subordinates,
- Pets – Guinea Pigs, Cat, Dog, Hamster, Fish, etc.

As you can see, the list is long and could be longer. Each category can be a TAPIN all by itself. You decide how many relationships you want to TAPIN. However, you choose to stroll through this platform, be prepared for the emotional work it will involve; you may have to deal with some of your deepest fears on this platform.

I challenge Travelers to remember that they are worthy of being loved just as they are; that it starts with self-love and the awareness they are enough all by themselves. If Travelers are in abusive relationships, either verbally or physically, I encourage them to seek professional help. All in all, each Traveler should deal with this platform by first seeking to love themselves. Love is a choice, and each Traveler must choose what works for them.

Types of Travelers on the Relationship Platform

- Dead end Travelers will arrive at this station ready to dump their current traveling companion, no longer willing to ride with them; this is definitely the last stop.

- Party-time Travelers who arrive tired, broken, and unwilling to rest may find themselves alone in this car. In a situationship without a commitment. Entertaining a friend with benefits or cheating with someone else's Traveler, often blaming others for their poor behavior.

- Weary Travelers may find time to party and brief rest as they locate other lifelong partiers just along for the ride.

- Commitment-ready Travelers will find their lifelong traveling companions and begin the trip of a lifetime.

- Seasoned Travelers already been on this journey with their traveling buddy and would not even consider taking a trip without them.

- None of the above

What is your Travel Type? What are your relationship needs?

_____

_____

_____

Whatever your current traveling style, you can plan a fantastic trip on this Platform. Here are a few samples for your TAPIN before you list your own:

Relationship TAPIN METHOD SAMPLES

T - Love Language – Knowing your partners Love language can add harmony. Go to www.5lovelanguages.com

A - Be clear on your desires and set your boundaries – abuse not acceptable. Read Boundaries by Dr. Henry Cloud & Dr. John Townsend

P - Get your house in order using the seven platforms in this book

I - Imagine yourself with your love of a lifetime

N - Nurture and respect the relationships you say are important

Reminder below use your journal to begin your TAPIN:

T	**Transformation**
A	**Announcement/Accountability**
P	**Preparation**
I	**Imagination**
N	**Nurture**

TAPIN TIPS

Practice Self-Love and Self-Care

Connect With Those You Love Often

NOTES:

"Know Who You Are. Know What You Want. Know What You Deserve. And Don't Settle For Less."

- Tony Gaskins.

5. Financial Platform

Now, more than ever, money management is essential. Looking for (and finding) opportunities to reduce and realign your spending will be necessary to maintain financial fitness.

There are many free and paid courses online geared to helping you make sound financial decisions. I became a Dave Ramsey Financial Peace University Coordinator after using the system to eliminate my debt. I wanted Travelers to:

"Live like nobody else, so they could live like nobody else."- Dave Ramsey

The devastation of financial mismanagement can affect every area of your life. I have witnessed the demise of many relationships because of poor money handling. Please be sure to take the time to access your money needs and reach out to creditors before they have to contact you. Many are making it easy to defer payments if you reach out in advance.

Travelers that fail to plan for the future by not participating in company 401k's or other retirement plans may be leaving money on the table. Travelers are encouraged to educate themselves on stocks, Certificates of Deposits (CD), Individual Retirement Accounts (IRA), and bonds. Travelers taking the time to become financially educated tend to be less stressed.

I started to help Travelers get serious about their finances. With so many Americans in a financial crisis, I wanted to provide practical advice to help them make better monetary choices. Although it is a stressful undertaking, the first step is acknowledging that you have a problem handling money. Money Matters and Motivation Monday is a resource I produce on Instagram and Facebook every Monday.

There was a time I was in so much debt I could not borrow money from my mama. I used to believe being in debt was typical. Now I live a debt-free lifestyle, teaching others how to do the same. How you view money determines if you live in lack, debt, or abundance. When you change your perspective, you change your reality. Are you ready to get financially fit?

Here is a sample of the information provided during a Money Matters Monday episode:

To become financially free happens $1.00 at a time. Not taking action still produces results. Here's a marvelous reminder If you had been saving money for the last six months this is what you could have had in the bank:

$0 a month x 6 = $0

$31 a month x 6 = $186

$59 a month x 6 = $354

$88 a month x 6 = $528

$121 a month x 6 = $726

$151 a month x 6 = $906

$302 a month x 6 = $1812

$1,510 a month x 6 = $9,060

$3,019 a month x 6 = $18,114

One dollar at a time is how you grow your wealth!

Take action! See what you can save in the next six months. Remember, Financial Fitness takes practice. Flex your money muscle, make those bank accounts grow.

Types of Travelers on the Financial Platform

- Travelers in debt so deep they see no way out but bankruptcy.
- Credit card juggling Travelers, running from creditors unwilling to change spending habits.

- Weary Travelers that have tried failed many times to become debt-free, still searching for a way out.

- Commitment-ready Travelers who are ready and open to a debt management practice.

- Seasoned Travelers who have already been on their personal money management journey living debt-free and would not consider living any other way.

- None of the above.

What is your Travel Type? What are your financial needs?

_____

_____

_____

_____

_____

Whatever your current traveling style, here are a few samples for your TAPIN before you list your own:

Financial TAPIN METHOD SAMPLES

T - Establish a financial management plan www.daveramsey.com

A - Conduct a money inventory and remove the financial Vampires from your Life

P - STOP SPENDING MONEY you don't have and take money management classes

I - Develop a plan for debt-free living. Imagine what Financial Freedom would feel like

N - Set financial boundaries and stick to them

Reminder below use your journal to begin your TAPIN:

T	Transformation
A	Announcement/Accountability
P	Preparation
I	Imagination
N	Nurture

TAPIN TIPS

Spend Money Responsibly

Cut Up and Limit Your Number Of Credit Cards

Have A Savings and Investment Plan

Educate Yourself And Your Family About Finances

Learn About Stocks:

https://www.bookworminvestmentclub.com

NOTES:

"If You Don't Get Serious About Your Money You Will Never Have Serious Money."

- Grant Cardone

6. Professional Platform

The Professional Platform can often leave people stuck. Lack of education, the opportunity for growth, and other factors can stall some travelers forward motion. This stop may require a detour to include a deboarding to attend a school or get additional certifications.

People all over the world go to jobs they hate every day. Our career choices can be a source of great joy or soul-crushing pain. When we are young, we are asked, "what do you want to be when you grow up?". Many kids say fireman, nurse, teacher, doctor, lawyer. I wanted to be the United States President, a lawyer, an entrepreneur, a movie star, a television host, and a writer. That is until I was eight years old and met my very first United States Marine. From that point on, I would be laser-focused on becoming a Marine.

I would start my first business, a candy store, at nine years old. At the age of twelve, I had my first paid job working at Buffundo Roofing Company. I made coffee for all the roofers, and by the time I left at age sixteen, I was doing payroll. I worked for DuPont Company in the mailroom during my senior year of high school, meeting all the engineers and learning about fabrics. At age seventeen, I entered the Marine Corps two days after graduation from high school.

I would spend twenty-plus years traveling the world doing what I love; helping people. Once I retired, I worked for thirteen years at a Hospital, most of which I held the Director of Environmental Services position. The point to all of this is you may not end up where you started. Seek out your dream job and reduce your stress. Life is to short to be sucked into professional purgatory.

Types of Travelers on the Professional Platform

- Travelers in careers that lack opportunity, with people they do not like.

- Travelers that jump from job train to job train with no clear career vision.

- Weary Travelers that have tried repeatedly but can't find employment.
- Commitment-ready Travelers ready to start their first job or a new one
- Seasoned Travelers who have already been on their professional journeys and are happy with their progress.
- None of the above

What is your Travel Type? What are your career needs?

_____
_____
_____
_____
_____
_____

Whatever your current traveling style, here are a few samples for your TAPIN before you list your own:

Professional TAPIN METHOD SAMPLES

T - Clarify career goals

A - Seek your dream job

P - Prepare your resume and take additional training as needed

I - Imagine your perfect job or career

N - Improve your professional development

Reminder below use your journal to begin your TAPIN:

T	Transformation
A	Announcement/Accountability
P	Preparation
I	Imagination
N	Nurture

TAPIN TIPS

Seek A Mentor

Stop Working In A Career Field You Hate

Find Employment That Brings You Joy

Volunteer In A Field Of Interest

Read Professional Development Books

Take Advantage Of All The Free Online Training

Embrace The Pivot

Network!!!!!!!!!!!!!!!!!!!!!!!!!!!!!!!!!!!!!!!

Do What You Love

NOTES:

"If You Don't Wake Up In The Morning Excited To Pick Up Where You Left Your Work Yesterday, You Have 't Found Your Calling Yet."

- Mike Wallace

7. Entrepreneurship Platform

Becoming an Entrepreneur is one of the scariest and most rewarding propositions that you will encounter. As the Owner/CEO, you will be responsible for the entire business. Travelers hitting this platform are sure to encounter detours. They must be relentless in the desire to achieve their goals. I ask them to examine why they want to go into business? No matter their reason for wanting to go into business, the final most important step is to acquire the proper knowledge to make their endeavor a success. I encourage Travelers to explore this route by seeking professional advice from organizations designed to support business startups. A few of those enterprises are:

- Local Colleges business centers designed to help with startups
- Small Business Association (SBA) www.SBA.gov
- Retired Executives are waiting to advise you for free at SCORE www.score.org
- Veterans, the Veterans Administration has excellent business resources for you at www.VA.gov

Types of Travelers on the Entrepreneur Platform

- Travelers wanting to start a new venture.
- Travelers who are serial entrepreneurs
- Weary Travelers who can't seem to get their business started
- Commitment-ready Travelers are ready and open to a franchise or new venture.
- Seasoned Travelers already a business founder/CEO.

What is your Travel Type? What are your Entrepreneurial needs?

_____

_____

_____

Whatever your current traveling style, here are a few samples for your TAPIN before you list your own:

Entrepreneur TAPIN METHOD SAMPLES

T - Starting/maintaining a business

A - Branding your business

P - Get funding, licenses, employees, training, and equipment

I - Plan your Grand Opening

N - Make sure you have reliable systems in place

Reminder below use your journal to begin your TAPIN:

T	Transformation	
A	Announcement/Accountability	
P	Preparation	
I	Imagination	
N	Nurture	

TAPIN TIPS

Do What You Love. Love What You Do!!!!!
Watch Interviews of Entrepreneurs at:
www.bit.ly/3s4vFC7

NOTES:

"Be Undeniably Good. No Marketing Effort Or Social Media Buzzword Can Be A Substitute For That."

-Anthony Volodkin

8. Veteran Services Platform

Becoming a Veteran is not an easy transition for many military members. Factor in not knowing what resources are available to you and your family, and you can see the dilemma. Figuring out how to do a resume, how to dress, what to say, and negotiating for pay can be overwhelming.

In chapter 16, I have provided a list of resources courtesy of the New England Veterans Chamber of Commerce that will get any Veteran or their family member well on the path to collecting benefits and helping them develop a Veteran owned business.

Be sure to read all the resources listed or pass this information to a Veteran you know.

Explore what is available to you and your family. There is information on how to get your student loans paid off, how to get one free year of LinkedIn, How to join Veterans Launching Ventures (VLV), to name a few. VLV was instrumental in my writing this book and completing my business plan.

Types of Travelers on the Veteran Services Platform

- Travelers just exiting the Military.
- Travelers who have served multiple tours of combat duty
- Weary Travelers suffering from service-connected PTSD /MST or both. Additionally, some with injuries unrelated to their service.
- Commitment-ready Travelers are ready and open to make the necessary change to navigate in the civilian community
- Seasoned Travelers already well integrated.
- None of the above.

What is your Travel Type? What are your Veteran Service's needs?

_____

_____

_____

Whatever your current traveling style, here are a few samples for your TAPIN before you list your own:

Veteran Services TAPIN METHOD SAMPLES

T - Educate yourself on your community and decide how you will show up

A - Determine what you want to do and get a Mentor

P - Seek out Resources. Find your States Veteran Services Office

I - Create a vision board or blueprint for your future

N - Maintain solid self-care plan for you and your family

Reminder below use your journal to begin your TAPIN:

T	**Transformation**
A	**Announcement/Accountability**
P	**Preparation**
I	**Imagination**
N	**Nurture**

TAPIN TIP

Never Give Up!!!!!!!!!!!!

Chapter 14

Well-Balanced Unapologetically Unstoppable Life

> *"A Well-Balanced Life is a lifetime commitment few people are willing to make." – Brenda Warren*

I wrote Soul Searching using the TAPIN Method to give you a foundation to build your own unique, well-balanced, unapologetically unstoppable life. Each step in the TAPIN Method required you to make a shift in your perception. Balance is now possible if you are willing to soul search and do the necessary work in the areas of need. It allows you to change the area(s) in your life that are not serving you well.

The eight examples given are not all-inclusive. They are a starting point for looking at your life and deciding what you want. What kind of experience do you choose to have? Yes, choose to have. If you discover you lack spiritually, mentally, physically, financially, professionally, entrepreneurially, or as a veteran, you now have tools to get you started on your journey to transformation.

By now, it should be clear living a well-balanced, unapologetically unstoppable life and creating a pattern of living takes work. I used the TAPIN Method for years to teach others how to live their best lives. I finally took my advice.

Here is a tiny glimpse into the life I have designed for myself after I started Soul Searching using the TAPIN Method. I started with my faith. I got clear on what I believed and revisited my core values. I removed all toxic relationships and committed to only having healthy ones. My finances, fitness, and wellness came next as I became debt-free, improved my health, built self-care practices, and lost weight simultaneously. My mental health, weight loss, professional development, and entrepreneurship continue to be a work-in-progress. I seek counseling, acknowledge I do not have to be perfect, take classes, and build my business while I continue to soul search using the TAPIN Method.

To maintain your well-balanced, unapologetically unstoppable life, a pattern of living with action steps is crucial. You can use prayer, meditation, or the practice of your choice to build your faith. Begin educating yourself regarding finances, fitness, and wellness. Build solid relationships that are loving and supportive. You stop spending money you don't have while learning to invest and save. Develop a solid exercise and healthy eating plan. You practice self-care. You seek higher education for professional development or start your own business. If you are a Veteran, you search for resources you have earned to support you and your family. All these actions combined will give you the base to build the life you want.

A well-balanced, unapologetically unstoppable life is not perfect. It is different for everyone. You get to determine what that looks like for you. For me, a well-balanced, unapologetically unstoppable life is one I can live as my authentic self. It is aligning every area I choose to address, supported by my core beliefs. Designing your well-balanced, unapologetically unstoppable life is not a one-time exercise. It is an ongoing practice that will allow you to live your best life non-stop. I challenge you to design the life you desire to live. Create a pattern of living that brings you great joy. I dare you!!!!

NOTES:

_____

_____

_____

NOTES:

NOTES:

Chapter 15

Finding Your Voice

> *"No one can silence your voice unless you allow it"*
> *– Brenda Warren*

For years I sat quietly in the back of the train. Afraid of moving forward or backward through any of the Platforms. My engine was low on gas as I attempted to make everyone else happy before refueling. From the windows, I watched as the world passed me by. In my silence, I shrunk smaller and smaller with each perceived offense, real and imagined, until I became practically invisible. The TAPIN Method allowed me to speak up and speak out. If you have made it this far, you understand the journey. The truth is the journey never ends. It would help if you continued to let go of old thoughts that don't serve you and create new ones.

Each time you soul search and TAPIN, you will discover your voice getting more substantial. The world needs to hear what you have to say. It is more comfortable to sit back, watch, and wait. However, you will never find your voice until you get comfortable with being uncomfortable. Someone needs to hear your story, so they know theirs will make a difference. Before I go, let me tell you a part of my journey.

I grew up the oldest of three kids living in government housing. My circumstance to the outside world told a story of poverty and lack. The information I told myself would determine what role lack played in my life. My mother stressed the importance of abundant living, so the story I lived was different than what people perceived. You see, I've always known a few vital universal truths that have allowed me to never live in a whole lack mentality. I believe if you apply them to your journey, you, too, can TAPIN to live abundantly.

I learned over the years that prosperity is so much more than finances. Your mind, body, and soul's well-being all contribute to prosperous living. The following list has grown and decreased for me when needed. This list can and should be modified to ensure personalization by any Traveler that uses it. I believe most of the bullets on this list will be familiar. As the saying goes, "there is nothing new under the sun." So what are some of the Prosperity Principles you should remember?

You Are A Designer's Original – Originals are always more valuable than a copy. No one can be better at being you than you.

You Were Created To Do Great Things – Find your purpose; it lays in your passion. To find your passion, you must seek out the one thing you would continually do even if you did not receive compensation.

Honesty Is The Best Policy – Your word must be your bond. A double-minded person cannot be trusted.

You Were Meant To Serve And Not Just To Be Serviced – Always look for ways to add value, not just take it.

Do For Others What You Would Like Them To Do For You – Treat everyone with respect.

You Have The Ability To Change Your Situation – Never make temporary problems permanent.

Don't Reinvent The Wheel – Find good mentors in the areas you want to succeed in and follow their lead. Success leaves clues!

Know The Rules – Learn how systems operate and make adjustments as necessary.

Be A Continual Learner - There will always be something you do not know. Let go of your ego. You are worth your investment.

Visualize Your Dreams - You will not pursue what you can not see.

Never Let Other People Stop Your Dreams - Write your vision and make it plain.

Set Goals For Yourself – Action plans are useless if you never move to achieve them. Do first things first. When you do what is necessary and not what is convenient, you will succeed. Note: sometimes goals change, don't be afraid to surrender old goals.

Be Time-Conscious - How you spend your time will determine your wealth; spiritually, physically, emotionally, and monetarily. Your actions will reveal to people if you value their time and yours.

If You Are Unwilling To Ask For What You Want, How Can You Expect to Receive It? – Please get a backbone and speak up! No won't kill you, and yes could change your Life.

Dress For Where You Are Going - Protocol matters and your attire will often determine the respect you receive. Don't show up to a black-tie event in a bathing suit. You will get noticed, but you will not garner respect.

Keep Your Inner Circle Small – The people you give access to your life determine the type of counsel you will receive. Be sure these people are qualified to speak into your life.

Give – Set aside a portion of your time and finances, always ensuring it benefits someone else.

Using the list above is the beginning of having an abundance mindset. Additionally, you need to decide what, if anything, is lacking in your life. Soul Searching and the TAPIN Method will help you clarify what lack is to you. It will help you determine what actions are needed to eradicate it from your thinking. The way you think about scarcity and any other issue in your life will guide your actions. Gain knowledge regarding the areas of your life you feel need to be adjusted to prevent deficiency.

We have access to more information and people than ever before in today's world. Many people want to live a prosperous existence but are unwilling to do even one of the things listed above. Some Travelers, citing lack of time, money, and/or discipline (to name a few) as barriers to achieving their desired outcome, will always be stuck in the station. I have often heard the saying, "*Knowledge is power,*" quoted in training seminars. I wholeheartedly disagree with that statement. I contend knowledge is only potential power. Why do I say potential power, you may ask? Currently, we have excessive knowledge about diet, exercise, and nutrition in America. According to stateofobesity.org, as of 2020, obesity continues to exceed 35 percent in five states and tops 30 percent in 25 states. You may know it, but it will be of no value if not applied.

You will need to decide never to allow other people or your circumstances to define your level of abundance. Steer clear of the naysayers willing to see lack where you see plenty. You must establish in your mind that you choose to determine your wealth in all areas of your life. Choose wisley and choose to live the TAPIN Method!!!! The choices you make today will be the reality you live in tomorrow.

NOTES:

_____

_____

_____

_____

_____

_____

_____

SOUL SEARCHING USING THE TAPIN METHOD

Veterans

We Are Stronger Learning From Each Other

GySgt Brenda Warren, USMC (Ret)

"Friends may come, friends may go, but our military-connection is forever."
     -Lisa Ducharme

Chapter 16

My Fellow Veterans

> *"I Plan To Show up Daily, that is how I will prevent myself from becoming another unnecessary silence."* –*Brenda Warren*

I joined the Marine Corps two days after my high school graduation in June 1980 and was blessed to travel all over the world for twenty-plus years. Upon retirement, I had no idea of the resources available to me. It took me **nineteen** years to discover all the amazing veterans' resources out there for me. A chance meeting with retired fellow veteran Lisa Ducharme, Executive Director of the New England Veterans Chamber of Commerce (NEVCC), www.nevcc.org, would change the trajectory of my business and also the way I viewed veteran's resources. Had I known about these resources, I could have saved myself both time and drama. I hope you will find these helpful.

Many veterans are unaware of the many resources available to them and their family members. Often programs go unused simply due to lack of knowledge on the part of the Veteran. The following resources have been complied and graciously provided by Lisa Ducharme. It is my sincere hope you will pass this information onto a Veteran or Veteran's family member you know.

This section has been broken down into two sections; Veteran Resources and Veteran Entrepreneurs and Business Owners (and their families). Always reach out to your Veteran Service Officer in your state or town, it is always best to get to know them before you need them.

Veteran Resources:

- Many veterans don't realize they are veterans if you served in the National Guard, Reserves or Active Duty military, and aren't sure, how to apply for a **Veterans Identification Card**. https://www.va.gov/records/get-veteran-id-cards/vic/

- **Center for Women Veterans (CWV)** https://www.va.gov/womenvet/ they have a call center the staff is trained to provide women Veterans, their families, and caregivers about VA services and resources. We are ready to respond to your concerns. The call is free, and you can call as often as you like until you have the answers to your questions.
  https://www.womenshealth.va.gov/WOMENSHEALTH/ProgramOverview/wvcc.asp

- In June they had a Women Veterans Forum, slides: https://www.va.gov/womenvet/docs/slidesDepSecWomenVeteransForum-20200623.pdf

- **National Parks – Free Access Pass for Service Disabled Veterans** - Many Veterans, with a service connected disability rating, are entering Federal recreation lands and national parks for free with lifetime access pass https://www.blogs.va.gov/VAntage/60590/disabled-veterans-eligible-free-national-park-service-lifetime-access-pass/

- **American Corporate Partners** This is a non-profit that matches veterans with mentors from Fortune 500 companies. The mentorships last for an entire year, and during that time veterans learn how to take their military experience and translate it into the corporate world. https://www.acp-usa.org/

- **AAFES** The Exchange—the Department of Defense's oldest and largest military retailer—is honored to serve all honorably discharged Veterans with a lifelong online military exchange shopping benefit.
  https://www.shopmyexchange.com/veterans

- **Post 9/11 GI Bill –** Many veterans who separated before 2009 do not realize they may be entitled to the Post 9/11 GI

Bill. For those who separated prior to January 2013, the Post 9/11 GI Bill benefits generally expire after 15 years, they are expiring everyday. For those who had Chapter 30, the MGIB-AD, their benefits expired after 10 years, but they may be eligible for the Post 9/11 GI Bill. So those who served should check it out: https://www.va.gov/education/how-to-apply/

- **LinkedIn Premium** 1 year free premium subscription for Military and Veterans: https://linkedinforgood.linkedin.com/programs/veterans/premiumform

- 1 year free premium link for military spouses: https://linkedinforgood.linkedin.com/programs/veterans/milspouses

- **Military/Veteran Caregivers and Fry Scholars**

  - To request a LinkedIn Premium upgrade, **caregivers** should email their full name and the full name of the veteran for whom they are caring to CaregiverLinkedIn.VBANYN@va.gov

  - **Fry Scholars** should email a request with their full name and contact information to 223D.VBAVACO@va.gov

- **PATRIOTlink** – Guides you to vetted, direct, cost-free services right at your fingertips. https://www.blogs.va.gov/VAntage/71957/free-resources-code-support-partiotlink/

- **Caregivers** – Many Service Disabled veterans have caregivers, and they need assistance too! **Hidden Heroes** https://hiddenheroes.org/

- **VA Caregiver Program** - Family caregivers play an important role in caring for the Veteran at home and in the community. There are 2 programs, the Comprehensive program is opening up to our WWII, Korean and Vietnam Veterans will be able to apply after the official launch date

(October) to find your VA Caregiver:
https://www.caregiver.va.gov/support/New_CSC_Page.asp

- ➢ Go to **Rosie Network's** to verify your military affiliation Rosie Network's no-cost, online process via GovX ID and by adding the "Veteran-Led" attribute to your Business Profile on Google. https://rosieslist.org/

- ➢ Rosie's List has launched its online eCommerce platform – the Marketplace for it's members now have the option of incorporating a **FREE shopping cart** into their profile page up to 10 products. https://rosieslist.org/ecwid-cart.php

NOTES:

SOUL SEARCHING USING THE TAPIN METHOD

Veteran Entrepreneurs and Business Owners (and their families):

Military, Veteran and Family member business leaders share their tips and strategies for military-connected businesses that you can apply to your business immediately:

- **Service2CEO** for transitioning service members, veterans and military spouses looking to launch and/or grow a small business. Graduates of Service2CEO become part of our national Alumni and participate in monthly masterclasses and networking opportunities.
  https://therosienetwork.org/service2ceo

- **Veteran Business Outreach Centers (VBOC)** were established by the SBA to help our veteran owned businesses, and they are generally not located in the SBA office, so make sure you check them out. https://www.sba.gov/about-sba/sba-locations/headquarters-offices/office-veterans-business-development/office-veterans-business-development-resources

- **Veteran Business Project** - If you are thinking about buying or at some point selling your business, the Veteran Business Project is a great place to start.
  https://veteranbusinessproject.org/

- If you use **LinkedIn**, there is a PDF I like, the LinkedIn Pages Playbook for businesses.
  https://business.linkedin.com/content/dam/me/business/en-us/marketing-solutions/cx/2018/pdfs/linkedin-pages-playbook.pdf

- If you are a Veteran or family member run business and are looking at expanding, check out **VETERAN**'s free "Streetwise MBA program" Free of tuition, this program is a six month VETRN program based on a course in strategic business planning, business cash flow and financial management, and is a collaboration with Interise, the developer of the highly successful, award winning "StreetWise MBA" program. https://vetrn.org

- ➤ There are many websites that ask Veterans to **post business information**, so people can find you/ Their search tools make it easy to find veteran owned businesses:

    - Rosie's List: https://rosieslist.org/

    - Veteran Owned Business: https://www.veteranownedbusiness.com/

    - Buy Veteran https://www.buyveteran.com/

- ➤ **Veteran or Service Disabled Veteran Certifications** there are a variety of certifications, but if you want to get certified through the VA, you can get assistance from your Local Procurement Technical Assistance Centers (PTACs), your SBA offices can connect you with your PTAC. For specific requirements:
  https://www.va.gov/osdbu/verification/index.asp

- ➤ **Veterans Launching Ventures** a FDU Rothman Veterans Program - Entrepreneur Certificate program, Fairleigh Dickinson University (FDU). Free to veterans and their family members (spouse and children) all eras.
  https://www.fdu.edu/academics/centers-institutes/rothman/veterans-launching-ventures/

- ➤ **Patriot Boot Camp (PBC)** Free 3-Day Technology Entrepreneurship Training. For aspiring technology entrepreneurs, Patriot Boot Camp (PBC) is a shorter, more condensed alternative. Since starting in 2012, PBC has held 9 programs in 7 cities and trained over 550 veterans, active-duty members, and spouses. PBC historically hosts 2-3 events per year, including two intensive 3-day entrepreneurship bootcamps and an alumni conference.
  https://patriotbootcamp.org/

- ➤ **Entrepreneurship Bootcamp for Veterans (EBV)**
  Cutting edge entrepreneurship training program teaching the

steps and stages of business creation and business management, with a tailored emphasis on the unique challenges and opportunities associated with being a veteran business owner. https://ivmf.syracuse.edu/

- ➢ **Veteran Institute for Procurement (VIP)** National Center for VIP is a veteran entrepreneurship program that specifically addresses federal procurement. VIP offers a platform with three (3) training programs to assist our veterans. VIP GROW is our core curriculum which assists companies in developing strategies to expand and operate within the federal marketplace. VIP START program is for companies wanting to enter the federal market and become procurement ready. https://www.nationalvip.org/

- ➢ **VetToCEO** Free 7-week "Mini Entrepreneurship MBA." A Georgia-based non-profit, offers a free 7-week online program called "Entrepreneurship for Transitioning Warriors". http://www.vettoceo.org/

- ➢ **Bunker Launch Lab online**- Free Online educational platform for the military-connected community who want to start their own business.
https://www.bunkeronline.org/launch-lab-online

- ➢ **American Corporate Partners** This is a non-profit that matches veterans with mentors from Fortune 500 companies. The mentorships last for an entire year, and during that time veterans learn how to take their military experience and translate it into the corporate world. https://www.acp-usa.org/

- ➢ Consider **Pitch competitions**. An example is Bob Evans Our Farm Salutes, they hold an annual pitch competition, but you create a video and pitch your business idea.
https://www.bobevansgrocery.com/our-story/our-farm-salutes/

- ➢ **Caregivers** – Many Service Disabled Veteran business owners have caregivers, and they need assistance too! https://hiddenheroes.org/

- ➢ If you are a military-connected business you should reach out to your local **Veterans Chamber of Commerce** for veteran specific resources.

    - If you are in a NE state, that would be the NEVCC. www.NEVCC.org

    - We are working on establishing a Chamber in each state

    - To find a Veterans Chamber in your state: **United States Veterans Chamber of Commerce**: www.USVCC.org

- ➢ **U.S. Small Business Administration (SBA)** continues to help small business owners and entrepreneurs pursue the American dream. The SBA is the only cabinet-level federal agency fully dedicated to small business and provides counseling, capital, and contracting expertise as the nation's only go-to resource and voice for small businesses. https://www.sba.gov/

- ➢ Reach out to your **Small Business Development Centers (SBDC)** at any stage in your business. https://americassbdc.org

- ➢ **SCORE** has a lot of resources, but the one I provide the link for the most is the financial templates: https://www.score.org/resource/business-planning-financial-statements-template-gallery

- ➢ **Fiverr** is one of my favorite resources for everything! If you want a jingle created, you can get it done. We did ours for $50 by Customdrumloops www.Fiverr.com

- ➢ When thinking about headlines for an article, a great resource is the **simple writing system**. https://simplewritingsystem.com/?cookieUUID=538e6670-7fa5-4b57-adf9-d354ca302797

- ➢ **Photos** – if you need a photo, there are 2 great websites for FREE royalty free photos: https://pixabay.com/ if you like

- word art, check out johnhain pieces and https://unsplash.com/

- **Legal Assistance** – Many Law Schools will assist you in setting up a business, many have law clinics for businesses at no charge.

- If you are a non-profit, create an account on **AmazonSmile**. Amazon donates 0.5% of the price of eligible AmazonSmile purchases to the charitable organizations selected by the customer. Non-profits can register to generate donations to their organization. https://org.amazon.com

- **PostPlanner** – If you are new to Social Media, and have a Facebook and/or Twitter account, for $3.00 a month you can schedule posts and use posts that are already created. It's a quick and easy way to start a social media presence. https://www.postplanner.com/

- **Free Power Breath Virtual Meditation Workshop** - a mind-body resilience-building program for returning veterans. It offers practical breath-based tools that decrease the stress, anxiety and sleep problems that many returning veterans experience.
https://projectwelcomehometroops.org/powerbreath-workshop/

- **New Politics Academy** – Free program, New Politics Leadership Academy is a nonpartisan nonprofit organization dedicated to recruiting and supporting servant leaders to serve through politics. service by jumping into the political arena. https://www.newpoliticsacademy.org/

- **Together We Served** -Find your battle buddies https://join.togetherweserved.com/va through unit pages https://blogs.va.gov/VAntage/73552/togetherserved-provides-virtual-base-connectingveterans/

NOTES:

ABOUT THE AUTHOR

Best Selling Author Brenda Warren, The Soulutionist, has been known for years as the voice for the voiceless. Her willingness to speak out for the under-heard was well known. As a retired United States Marine with over twenty years of active-duty service, she strongly advocates for veterans. Brenda is a serial entrepreneur. She has been founding successful businesses in the Candy, Fashion, Sewing, Financial, and Relationship industries starting at nine years old.

Brenda traveled the world for over thirty-three years teaching others about leadership, self-care, cultivating healthy relationships, and spiritual growth. Brenda's teachings would be put to the test when she had a mental breakdown in 2013 while serving as the Director of Environmental Services at a hospital in Goldsboro, North Carolina. Diagnosed with Post-Traumatic Stress Disorder (PTSD) and Military Sexual Trauma (MST) in 2011, she was overmedicated, unheard by doctors and family. Their one size fits all approach to her care left her desperate to find her voice and solutions to her ongoing issues, including chronic pain disorders.

Brenda now teaches others using a mind, body, and soul approach to Show Up and Power Up in their unique way to live a well-balanced, unapologetically unstoppable life. She is passionate about helping veterans and others find their voices and preventing another unnecessary silence. Brenda believes it is more important to help others find their authentic voice. She shares her message globally online, at churches, and other organizations across the country. Brenda has appeared on the Tanya Bardo Angels United Podcast, Life Laughter Happiness Podcast, Second Chance Athletes Podcast, The Miss Francois Show, The Brooklyn Cafe TV show. She Hosted The Editor's Desk for Amp Media Productions TV Show. At the time of this writing, Brenda is the Host of the YouTube Show Talk To Me and is a Mental Fitness Coach.

BONUS

Create Your Story with A Vision Board

You've probably heard of vision boards, but have you ever made or used one? A vision board is essentially a large poster that you construct to help you achieve your goals. It contains pictures that represent your goals.

For example, during your TAPIN if you dreamed of losing weight, you might include photos of the gyms, exercise equipment, healthy meals, and sample pictures of someone that has achieved the look you want to acquire.

It might sound like silly new-age nonsense, but a vision board can be useful!

Consider what a vision board does for you:

- It forces you to decide on your goals.
- It requires you to review your goals daily.
- It sensitizes you to opportunities that aid in the achievement of your goals.

However, it does not magically make the objects of your desire appear in your life without any work on your part. You'll still have to work, but a vision board can be invaluable.

Use these strategies to create your vision board:

1. **Decide what you want to be, do, and have.** This is one of the primary reasons that vision boards can be so effective. They require you to think about what you want and to make a few choices.

- Review your soul searching exercise. **choose the things and experiences that are most important to you.**

- Be bold. If your vision board doesn't inspire you, it won't be effective.

2. **Find visual images that represent what you want to be, do, and have.** You can look online or in magazines. What's important is that you have the same feeling when you look at the photo as you do when you think about that thing. The sensations should match.

3. **Arrange your vision board in a way that pleases you.** You can be orderly or use more of a collage style. Each objective can have its own board, or everything can be combined on a single board. There are no rules. **Follow your instincts and allow your creativity to flow.**

4. **Hang your vision board where you'll see it frequently.** A vision board sitting in the closet isn't of much use. Consider your daily activities and put your vision board where you'll see it most frequently.

5. **Take a photo of your vision board.** Use your phone and take a photo. That way, you'll have it wherever you go. You can always pull out your phone and view your board.

6. **Start and end your day with your vision board.** At the very least, **take a long look at your vision board when you first wake up and when you go to bed.** You might need to rely on a photo if your vision board isn't in your home.

7. **Use a process to view your vision board.** Think about each goal you have and look at the photos that represent those goals. Allow yourself to feel excited about achieving that goal. Feel yourself at your goal weight, or whatever accomplishing the goal you set for yourself.

- Go through each item on your vision board and experience success in your mind.

8. **Be persistent.** Vision boards don't work overnight, but they do work. They remind you of your goals and keep them at the forefront of your mind. **They allow you to experience positive feelings with regards to achieving your goals.** Keep at it.

9. **Take action.** Avoid the belief that your weight will magically fall off. You still have the responsibility to take action. Using your vision board will allow you to notice more opportunities. Take advantage of them.

Start your first vision board today and use it daily. **There's nothing to lose.** Making a vision board can be fun. If you have any children in your life, they'd love to help! A vision board can be more powerful than you think.

ADDITIONAL RESOURCES

Continue your Soul Search and TAPIN with the Digital Recourses from The Soulutionist, Brenda Warren!

Visit www.brendathesoulutionist.com to download them **FREE**...... and begin enjoying tools that will help you live a well-balanced **Unapologetically Unstoppable Life --- Today!**

Made in the USA
Middletown, DE
05 November 2024